THE HIRING COMPASS

How to Navigate the Talent Pool Paradox and Avoid Hiring Shipwrecks

By Mark Debinski

www.bluewateradvisory.com

To my wife Janet and our daughters Rebecca and Delaney, whose unconditional love and support serve as the wind in my sails, as well as the lighthouse, guiding me home from each journey.

TABLE OF CONTENTS

FOREWORD

By Bill J. Bonnstetter
Chairman,
Target Training International, Ltd. &
TTI Success Insights North America

I first met Mark Debinski three years ago when, already an accomplished business executive, he began working with Target Training International, Ltd.'s (TTI) tools for a new business he was launching. Utilizing our patented job benchmarking as well as other TTI solutions, Mark informed me he was set upon providing a better option in the recruiting industry. Unlike too many other entrepreneurs with high hopes, I recognized Mark as an individual who would be able to harness the power of his experience, skills and talents, couple them with our reliable, researched assessments, and succeed in his endeavor. I was confident Mark's approach to the selection market would bring much-needed integrity to the field. I was sure that, as an end result, his unique approach would help businesses select better employees and help individuals find their perfect job match.

Hiring seems to be a simple process. But my more than 30 years in the assessment, selection and human capital industry has proved that it is anything but simple. Selection is complicated, mostly by our own biases and blind sides. No leader wants to hire someone who does not perform well in his or her job. Having a team filled with bright, extraordinarily talented individuals only makes a leader stronger, better and more powerful. Yet, leaders and hiring managers are still challenged when hiring and we've all made bad hires at one time or another. Why is that the case? What are the common issues that keep us from hiring superior performers? "The Hiring Compass" provides great insight.

Most people can formulate a first impression of a person in 30 seconds or less. This impression springs from our biases, stored in our subconscious. So we can like or dislike a potential employee even before the interview has started. Without understanding our biases, many people are hired because the interviewer simply liked them. That is more like a personality contest than a hiring process.

It was this awareness that led my team at TTI and me to create our patented job benchmarking process in 2007. The process, which Mark is an expert in implementing for his very successful clientele, begins by letting the job speak. That is the start of all hiring. If you do not begin the process to hire an amazing employee with a fresh look at what the job you are hiring for actually entails, the entire process is likely doomed from the start. Creating a job benchmark before hiring is not a corner to cut — it's vital to the success of the hire. So, how do leaders avoid falling victim to these hiring pitfalls? A good first step is to read "The Hiring Compass."

After reading what Mark has put together here, it is clear I was correct in my initial impression and that he has found great success with his strategic approach to selection. But more than that, in "The Hiring Compass," he goes further, providing a clear, concise map of this selection process so that others may also make use of it and become more aware of the reality of the recruiting and selection industry. To me, that is going above and beyond. I'm thrilled Mark has not shied away from exposing the bad actors and poor selection techniques that exist within the market. This is the only way there can be healthy growth and stability in the industry.

Anyone involved in the hiring of new talent will find "The Hiring Compass" extremely helpful in his or her work. It will provide fresh perspective about the particular hiring dynamics at play in the 21st century, as well as intelligent analysis of how best to attack those challenges and, therefore, to hire superior performers — safely and effectively. I recommend it.

CHAPTER 1

Why Really Smart People Make Really Bad Hiring Decisions

Looking for a terrific conversation-starter to use at your next professional networking event? After you exchange pleasantries and establish rapport, smile and say, "Tell me about a memorable hiring mistake."

Then, just listen. Try this a few times and you will be amazed at the stories shared. Almost anyone who has been in the workforce for any period of time will have a story: some funny, some not so funny, others ending in costly lawsuits, settlements, career derailments or even worse.

The point of this exercise is not to cast blame, open up old wounds or establish a power stance over the person with whom you are speaking. Instead, the reason for the discussion is to shed light on an often unspoken phenomenon — that really smart people (and really smart companies) often make really bad hiring decisions.

Why is this and what's the big deal? We will address the "the big deal" in detail in subsequent chapters. The executive sum-

"So, why do really smart people and really smart companies make really bad hiring decisions?"

mary answer to "what's the big deal?" is that hiring mistakes rack up serious hard costs, and more importantly, the widespread wake and negative ripple effect they cause can profoundly impact your business. From lost productivity, to hits on management credibility and morale in general, from the emotional toll to career opportunity losses, the costs and impacts of a hiring mistake are significant.

So, why do really smart people and really smart companies make really bad hiring decisions? There are myriad reasons for poor hiring decisions, and our research and experience reveal the following to be primary contributors. I refer to these errors as the Top Ten Shipwrecks of Hiring Mistakes, because the cost of a bad hire can easily equate to the price tag of your dream vacation condo (more on that later).

No one starts out a talent search hoping to hire someone who is a bad fit for the job. Yet, bad hires are extremely common. Despite our best intentions, we still hire poorly. Therefore, we must look deeper to uncover what is leading to these bad hires — and how we may be knowingly and unknowingly contributing to poor hiring decisions.

History and research tell us our unconscious plays a role. Every person is unconsciously motivated by six primary motivators, and each — or a combination thereof — can heavily influence the way we view the world. These primary motivators (theoretical, utilitarian, aesthetic, social, individualistic, traditional) and the ways these unconscious biases can get in the way of interviewing and hiring decisions are:

Theoretical - Theoretically motivated people are driven toward continuous learning and research. They tend to enjoy hearty dialogue, debate and "what-ifs." A candidate who exhibits similar tendencies in an interview can score big points with a high-theoretical. This can be a win-win if the job at hand requires such theoretical traits and motivation. However, if the job does not require research, theory exploration, new idea generation, etc., an interviewer's theoretical bias could result in the interviewer passing up good candidates for the position. It could also result in a hiring recommendation because the candidate exhibits similar theoretical values, regardless of the specific job requirements.

Utilitarian - A utilitarian is driven by results, achieving goals, setting higher goals and achieving them. Utilitarians are also fiercely protective of their time, driven to make the most of it. As an example, an interviewee who pauses to collect his or her thoughts, is slightly long-winded, or repeats themselves for clarity or to make a point, may quickly disengage a high-utilitarian interviewer. Conversely, a candidate whose remarks are short and to the point may ring loudly with the high utilitarian. The unconscious bias exists, and the utilitarian nature and need of the specific job, can influence the decision or hiring recommendation either positively or negatively.

Aesthetic - An aesthetic is driven toward and influenced by beauty, harmony and balance. While some jobs require strong aesthetic motivation (such as architects, graphic artists, and environmentalists), a high- or low-aesthetic motivator poses significant bias risk on the part of the interviewer. For example, a high-aesthetic CEO of a design firm may be put off by a hard-charging salesperson or a no nonsense finance manager; however, that may be exactly what the firm needs! One business owner with whom we worked to re-engineer his firm's hiring process told us in our initial meeting that after conducting an interview, he always walked the candidate to his or her car, confident he could learn more about the candidate by their car than the interview process. He proudly recounted how many candidates he eliminated from the screening process based upon the condition of their car. Who knows how many good hires he missed! And what about the candidate who may have taken someone else's car on interview day and had their fate sealed (positively or negatively) based on a messy friend's jalopy?

Social - Not to be confused with a social butterfly, a socially motivated individual is one who is motivated by serving others, helping, and otherwise giving back to society. This value is admirable and many of society's most valuable contributors are socially driven, including many who work for non-profits, academia, and healthcare, among others. A high-socially motivated person may unconsciously discount candidates who don't exhibit the same passion for giving back, and thereby pass on potentially great hires. Conversely, this bias may cause the interviewer to be overly drawn towards candidates who embody similar values, sometimes outweighing whether the candidate is actually best qualified for the position!

Individualistic - Often referred to as political, the individualistically motivated values power and visibility. This is not necessarily a bad thing, so long as the drive is balanced by morals and a healthy emotional intelligence. The bias risk may present itself, however, in two ways:

1. A high-individualistic interviewer may undervalue a candidate who does not display a certain level of the same value.

2. In some cases, a high-individualistic interviewer may actually feel threatened by a high-individualistic candidate. In this "not in my sandbox" scenario, excellent candidates can be

passed over due to the subconscious threat the individualistic interviewer feels, resulting in a milquetoast, less-than-optimal hire.

Traditional - This motivator may present the highest of the bias risks. Traditionally motivated people adhere to a belief system. While often religious, the valued belief system could be of many other types. Sometimes entire organizations are made up primarily of people with like-minded belief systems. Hence, the bias may be amplified and good candidates may be subconsciously passed over because they don't quite fit. Additionally, a traditionally motivated organization or interviewer may sometimes scare off ideal candidates due to the zeal with which they hold their beliefs. It should be noted, however, that forward-thinking organizations have been able to achieve some balance between maintaining the traditional values of the organization and embracing the diversity that exists within today's workplace. We are proud to have worked with and witnessed this in practice with a century-old faith-based organization with over 13,000 employees, which has deliberately broadened its view to accept those of all faiths.

Do you see yourself in any of these motivators? Can you identify how you or your hiring manager may have allowed these motivators to affect hiring?

Recognizing our own role in bad hiring is the first step of unraveling the effects a bad hire can have: the true cost of hiring shipwrecks. The second step is to understand the ten most common hiring mistakes people make and how poor hires can be detrimental to businesses for years beyond the one-time event of hiring. Those who wish to improve their hiring must also understand current hiring conditions and the effects of the Talent Pool Paradox as well as best practices within the field of recruiting. Finally, learning the steps of the most advantageous search and selection hiring method will illustrate the return on investment you will enjoy if you choose to use such a researched, deliberate and time-tested hiring process.

Learning more about hiring is highly valuable — not just to you as an individual, but also to your company and future business operations. Since we often learn better by hearing the real-life examples of bad hires, we also present these throughout "The Hiring Compass" as a way of orienting the journey to better hiring.

Unwanted Culture Shift Spins Ship Off-Course

While hiring a CFO for my company, I interviewed an individual who was proposing a number of changes in the organization. In fact, this candidate made the approval and implementation of these changes a requirement to her accepting the position. Complicating matters was the number of credentials the applicant had and the fact that I had paid a search firm a large sum of money to recruit for the position. I'm not precisely sure why, but I disregarded my negative gut feelings and moved forward despite my major reservations. Even though I had a sense during the hiring process that hiring her would be a mistake, she was hired.

Very rapidly, this individual severely damaged the culture of my company, which I had worked incredibly hard to establish. She nearly caused me a lawsuit or two. She talked a big game, while outsourcing many things she should have done herself. Eventually, I fired her. I've never regretted that decision, but the choice to hire her still irks me.

*It was definitely a learning experience
— I learned never to let anyone change
the core of the company I worked so hard
to build. In my case, the changes I had
agreed to nearly lead to the destruction of
my business. While it was a difficult experience, I ultimately realized how vital my
company's culture is to me, to my employees and to the success of the business.*

CHAPTER 2

The True Cost of a Hiring Mistake

Hiring mistakes are very costly. Almost all companies in all parts of the world make hiring mistakes. A study released by Career-Builder in spring 2013 conducted by Harris Interactive© surveyed over 6,000 hiring managers and human resource professionals in the 10 countries with the highest gross domestic product. The study is one of the most recent to confirm the negative consequences of bad hires. More than half of the companies polled reported they had made hiring mistakes (defined as people who were a bad fit for the job or those who simply did not perform the job well — or both). Losses cited were both tangible and intangible, including measurable losses in revenue or productivity, or negative impacts to employee morale and client relations.

The study revealed general agreement that the financial impact of hiring mistakes are significant, with 27 percent of U.S. employers reporting a single bad hire cost more than $50,000. Moreover, it is widely believed the cost of a hiring mistake is grossly underestimated; many professionals believe the true cost of a hiring mistake to be somewhere between three and five times the failed position's annual salary. Even for an entry-level salary of $25,000, that could equate to $125,000.

The Costs Associated with Hiring Shipwrecks

Lost productivity - Whether your business is professional services, manufacturing, or one of a plethora of other industries, hiring mistakes often deal a serious blow to productivity. At a recent speaking engagement, one attendee estimated recent turnover at his firm had cost him over $500,000 in productivity and bonuses. John, a principal in a successful architectural firm, recalled he made the decision to hire two "superstars" from a competitor. Though the decision was admittedly against his better judgment because he had heard that these two gifted architects were also high maintenance, he was swayed by a few of his project managers. In addition to being high maintenance, the two new team members were also disruptive and political, creating silos among the current staff commonly referred to as "camps," in a nod to the popular show Survivor. Even though John made the decision to "regift

"Morale is almost 100 percent correlated to engagement."

to the field" both of the new hires within 90 days, the damage was done and productivity plummeted, causing the firm to miss key deliverable dates; hence, fourth quarter billings were delayed and the firm missed its goals for the year, which meant no bonuses.

Decrease in morale - A very common side effect, and often a compounding effect of hiring mistakes, is a decline in morale. This is particularly dangerous because it often goes undetected at first, while the negative wave spreads through employees and departments. Suddenly you find yourself talking people off ledges and lifting people up all at the same time.

Morale is almost 100 percent correlated to engagement. We define engagement as the level of discretionary effort one puts into their job — over and above the bare minimum. That is, just showing up and putting in a fair day's work for a fair day's pay does not necessarily mean someone is engaged. In its ongoing study of the American workplace, the Gallup organization polled over 25 million workers from 2010 to 2012 and found on average, only about one-third of all employees described themselves as engaged — that is, doing more than the bare minimum. Approximately half of the polled employees described themselves as disengaged. That is, half of the respondents reported showing up and doing the minimum to get by but no more. Here is the scary part — almost 20 percent of those employees polled described themselves as actively disengaged! As if it wasn't bad enough half of employees are coming to work and just sliding by, it turns out one in five are actively spreading negative energy throughout the organization, recruiting those on the fence to come over to the dark side.

The best way to envision engagement is to picture a schooner sailing to your ideal destination. If you captain a schooner with sails that are adequately filled (status quo, disengaged) you may be satisfied and believe you are making good time toward your destination. But, when you see a nearby vessel clipping across the waves with sails full to maximum capacity (engagement!) you realize your ship is not quite doing all it can. Now picture your sails with half the wind let out — the sails appear limp, listless, sagging in the breeze (active disengagement) and your schooner is going nowhere. Apply that picture to your organization and ask which ship you are sailing.

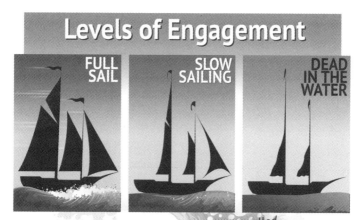

Levels of Engagement

FULL SAIL   SLOW SAILING   DEAD IN THE WATER

Almost 20% of those employees polled described themselves as actively disengaged!

We share the above statistics not to be dramatic, but to paint the stark picture of the usual state of things in the workplace and among employees. Even in the usual state, managers and owners have their hands full. Layering in a hiring mistake or two only exacerbates the active disengagement and ill will some employees harbor. On a positive note, however, improving your organization's hiring processes and reducing (or ideally eliminating) the number of hiring mistakes can have a profound and positive effect on morale and engagement throughout your entire organization. Now let's continue with our list of costs associated of hiring shipwrecks.

Lost sales - This is one of the most tangible costs of a hiring mistake. It's also often underestimated. Lost sales come in many forms and can have a compounding negative impact on your organization. The most obvious are the sales from your good customers and clients who tell you they have become disenchanted, annoyed — or worse — because of your hiring mistake. This could be a six-figure client whose material or equipment does not show up on time and causes delays to their project, or it could be the 157 paid subscription cancellations that pour in because of a surly call center employee. The latter may be harder to measure but of significant value nonetheless. Even more difficult to quantify are the should-have-been sales that never quite make it across the finish line and onto your books. These could be orders in the pipeline that suddenly dry up, or prospects you are almost certain to close that quietly go away. As an executive or business owner, it is likely in any given year, your organization loses hundreds of thousands of dollars in sales due to one or more hiring mistakes.

Cost of recruiting a replacement worker - When a hiring mistake comes to fruition and that person quits or you are forced to regift them to the field, the company is often left with a void that must be filled quickly in order to minimize damage and maintain momentum. This often requires heavy recruitment costs, whether from internal resources or outside recruitment services. In this case, it is incumbent upon you to do it right. These two suggestions should help toward that end: first, use some of the objective tools, such as assessments, outlined later in the book, and second, if using an outside recruitment firm, insist they use objectivity tools before candidates are put in front of you. Lastly, be sure to negotiate a placement guarantee with the outside recruitment firm, so if the newly placed candidate falls out within 90 days or so, the recruitment firm must replace the hire.

Opportunity cost - This is simply the cost of what should have been. Surely lost sales fall into this category; however, there are other opportunity costs firms face when a hiring mistake is made, depending upon the position that fails. For example, if the wrong person is hired to oversee a plant expansion with heavy capital investment, delays or failures in project delivery could result in expensive downtime, meeting deliverables and upholding forecasts based upon the expansion. Or if the wrong person is hired or promoted to oversee the merger of two organizations or a major cost-cutting initiative, the efficiencies gained from those efforts are not likely to come to fruition.

Legal, severance and risk mitigation costs - From past experience as an executive and as a consultant helping clients resolve hiring mistakes, this category can often represent the largest costs of a hiring mistake, often running between $10,000 to over $100,000. Depending upon the risk tolerance of the organization and their policies on handling sticky situations, some companies would rather surrender and be very generous in the exit package in order to avoid perceived exposure to legal action from the departing employee. Because every situation is unique and each organization tends to develop its own philosophy regarding departures and associated risk, we will neither judge nor condone the generous route. We will, however, bring it to light because it happens so often. Typically, to avoid potential open risk once an employee is terminated, companies are often generous in severance and other negotiated exit payments (extended insurance, guaranteed bonus, etc.) in order to receive a clean departure agreement waiving rights to any future claims. This philosophy often takes solace in the thought that spending $50,000 in order to save $100,000 in future exposure and legal costs is a good investment to put an issue to rest. But how many of these can any company afford, and how many of these must an organization absorb before someone makes proactive changes at the root cause — the hiring process?

Cost of corporate reputation - Damage to an organization's reputation as the result of a hiring mistake is difficult to measure but can be enormous. Most organizations realize this and will spend the time and resources for proper objective search and selection efforts for higher level managers. More often than not, however, we find a significant gap between the effort and objectivity spent on high-level positions compared to lower level positions. While we recognize it is not cost-efficient to treat every search like C-level searches, there are some easy and cost-effective tools and processes to upgrade search and selection efforts at even the lowest level of the organization. (We'll delve into these tools later in Chapter 7.)

Cost to the regifted worker - The last cost to highlight is the cost to the regifted worker. Of course we don't shed tears for those who blatantly violate policy and leave the company no choice but to show them the door in quick fashion. However, we quite commonly see situations where the statement, "it just wasn't working out" applies. In these situations the company is faced with many or all of the costs highlighted above, while the regifted employee faces loss of income, another notch on their résumé, a potentially tainted reputation for "failing," and the daunting task of a new job search. While it is difficult to put a value on it, the stress and anxiety that accompanies a termination or forced resignation can be extreme.

In summary, the costs associated with a hiring mistake are many. Often times, these costs fly under the radar and are overlooked when companies are scrambling to clean up a hire gone bad. But don't just take our word for it — try to identify the costs of hiring mistakes for yourself at your own company. Simply visit bluewateradvisory.com and click on the Cost of a Hiring Mistake Calculator link to calculate the cost to your company. Based on our professional experience, the opinion of 6,000 human resources and hiring professionals, and your own calculator figures, don't you agree there is value in learning and utilizing some of the many tools available to increase your chances for successful hires every time you hire?

Great Credentials, Terrible Captain

After three plus decades leading corporate marketing, I was nearing retirement and knew the firm needed a senior level external communications leader upon my departure. I learned at a national conference a respected communications professional was looking for a job. Julie had wonderful credentials: over 20 years of experience, national media relationships, MBA, registered architect and she was a marketing services fellow. Best of all, she was nice and got along well with people. The hiring process went smooth and Julie was named corporate communications director.

Within three months doubts began to surface. Julie was smart, she collaborated well, but she needed to be told what to do. The problem was there wasn't a senior executive who had national communications expertise when I retired. After a year, Julie was given a three-month notice and then terminated. The hiring error was mine. I made the assumption someone with great credentials who was well liked would also be a great leader.

CHAPTER 3

The Top Ten Shipwrecks of Hiring Mistakes

No one launches a business or accepts an executive position with the goal of incurring multiple unnecessary expenses. Yet, time and again, hires that end up being ship-wrecks cost companies three to five times the salary of the employee who did not work out. Not just that, these hires put at risk the reasons we go into business in the first place — to achieve success and to relish the spoils of our own success, whether those be the ability to travel, to give back to the community, to live in a luxurious home, or to purchase your dream vacation home in an ideal, relaxing locale. Using the calcula-tion of three- to five-times the employee's salary, hiring a shipwreck may equate to

"Yet, time and again, hires that end up being shipwrecks cost compa-nies three to five times the salary of the employ-ee who did not work out."

losing hundreds of thousands of dollars —
enough of a loss for you to kiss that dream
second home goodbye. To put the cost to our
dreams in perspective, we compare the cost
of hiring a shipwreck to the potential (lost)
investment in an about to be purchased
beachfront condo or vacation property.

HIRING SHIPWRECK #1
Beachfront Condo Goes Bye-bye:
My biases made me hire

It is only natural for interviewers and hiring managers to want to make some type of
connection with the person they are going to
hire for their organization. Ideally, the new
hire fits in well with the organization, and
finding some common ground during the
interview process typically supports the "fit"
ideal. However, while it is true a new employee will have a better chance of success and
job fulfillment in an organization in which
he or she is comfortable culture-wise, all too
often our conscious and unconscious biases
wrongly influence decision making during
the interview and hiring process.

As we discuss various biases to illustrate
how biases can negatively affect otherwise
good hiring, keep in mind here and throughout this book, we take the adamant stance

that bias toward any prospective employee due to race, gender, age, or protected class is not only illegal, it is wrong. We define bias as a natural leaning toward a given attribute, competency or other trait.

Human beings have two different types of bias — those that are conscious and those that are unconscious. If aware of the conscious biases, we are more effective at counteracting them, but both types can weigh heavily, influencing interview perceptions and hiring decisions. Let's discuss both in detail. A conscious bias is one we are aware of and often seeking to validate or invalidate during the interview process. The mindset of this bias is "if this person meets this expectation they have a better chance of succeeding in our organization." This can be true, but is not always — or even often — true. Moreover, people who let conscious biases come into play during the interview process often overlook some of the best candidates for the position because the candidate does not outwardly exhibit the trait the hiring manager is seeking.

One of the most overt examples that comes to mind is a fast growing company in the northeast that has always embraced a hard work ethic and sense of urgency — to the point that rushing (even running!) around the office and throughout the office campus is an honored tradition. Literally running into someone coming around a corner, or showing up to a meeting with beads of sweat on one's brow and perspiring, has been a long-honored and valued trait. Let's stop running and pause for a moment — while a sense of urgency toward one's job is typically a desired trait, is someone who runs doing a better job than someone who walks? And what about the person who may be perfect for the specific position, but may not be in prime physical shape? Or even worse, what about the prime candidate who has more overt physical limitations?

The purpose of this illustration is to strike some balance and create awareness between hiring people who will fit into and embrace strong company culture (which often has positive results), and letting an individual's or organization's conscious bias weigh too heavily in hiring decisions, which can have significant detrimental effects. Other conscious biases include giving undue weight to school or geographic pedigree, former company experience, and even sports team allegiances!

The unconscious bias presents a dual risk, as it is both harder to discern and also harder to overcome than the conscious bias. At least with the conscious bias, those with the understanding of the need for bias balance and adequate self-awareness can typically recognize when their bias may be weighing too heavily on a decision.

Unconscious bias, on the other hand, is a sticky wicket. After all, how we do maintain self-awareness and control something we are not even aware of? Take a look back at the first chapter to see if you can identify an underlying values and belief system — or paradigm — that resonates with your approach to hiring. This will help you become more familiar with your unconscious biases and therefore better able to consciously redress any imbalance they cause.

HIRING SHIPWRECK #2
The Bayside Condo Collapse: Self-mirroring mirage

Self-mirroring behavior is high on the list of tragic hire contributors. Self-mirroring refers to an influential person in the hiring decision who feels the best person for the job —any job— is someone just like them. We mostly see the self-mirroring monster rear its ugly head in three common scenarios:

A high ego rationalizes, "I'm good in my job; I'm good for this business. Naturally, the best thing I can do for this business is hire people just like me." Tragically, tenure does not trump ego. That is, we find this high-ego dysfunction at all levels of the organization.

Often well-intended though still inexcusable, inexperienced and untrained interviewers often "default" to self-mirroring simply because they don't know a better way. When in doubt, these newbies tend to lean toward someone similar to them, whether or not those attributes are good for the specific job for which they are interviewing. More inexcusable is the organization or manager who put this inexperienced hiring manager in a position to hire.

Job benchmarking refers to the process of diving deep into a job to the point of developing a list of core ideal attributes for a specific position. Benchmarks are very valuable and a key component to great hires and strong job fit, as they provide a target and map against which to objectively compare candidates. (We will explore job benchmarking in greater depth in a later chapter.) However, benchmarks are valuable only for the particular job for which they were performed. Often organizations try to stretch or repurpose a benchmark for one particular job across other jobs within the organization — hence, self-mirroring a position as opposed to a person, resulting in hiring misfits. Like a caulk gun in the hands of the untrained, benchmarking by those not professionally trained and lacking the appropriate assessment tools can yield messy results. That is, we have seen managers in organizations conduct their own watered-down versions of job benchmarks and then wonder why they ended up with watered down hiring results.

HIRING SHIPWRECK #3
Cabin in the Mountains Meltdown:
Rushing the slot

This is arguably the deadliest of the hiring mistake sins because: 1) it has the highest risk of failure, 2) it can be the most costly, and 3) it is the most avoidable. There are so many reasons for needing to rush to fill the slot (or slots) including unexpected turnover, high rate of growth that requires more bodies, staffing up for seasonal volume, etc. However, when companies are under pressure to fill slots, objectivity and established policies and processes are often set aside in the interest of the urgent matter at hand ("fill that position"), and the risk of a bad hire goes up exponentially. These hiring mistakes can be the most costly. Over and above the costly cleanup often associated with the other hiring mistakes, hiring under time pressure and when the objective guard is let down can let the wrong people in the door, resulting in theft and fraud, trade and customer confidentiality breaches, and more. The next time a colleague tells you, "I have just got to get this position filled and will take anyone," do them a favor and ask them, "Who has done the job before?" It is possible a more senior team member may need to retake the role while a permanent placement is found. You can also ask them, "If you had to pick one person to do this role, who would it be?" You will be surprised at the creativity this often generates.

HIRING SHIPWRECK #4
City Loft Letdown: Poor at interviewing, poor at hiring

It is only natural for people to want to be involved in the interviewing and hiring process, for many reasons. Being included in hiring presents the opportunity to weigh in on new team members, to glimpse other parts of the organization and to have a say when it comes to prospective employees in one's own department who may be direct reports. After all, there's something fun about helping someone pick out a new car. You get to kick someone else's new tires, comment on the pros and cons, and essentially add weight to a very expensive decision, without spending a dime yourself. Same goes for interviewing!

The danger lies, however, when you give the keys to someone who doesn't know how to drive. Bad things happen. Putting the untrained into the interviewing mix presents several areas of risk. First, the chances are great the untrained interviewer will fall prey to one of the other hiring mistakes. Next, compound the potential cost of the hiring mistake when the untrained interviewer says the wrong thing, causing a prime candidate to walk away, or even worse, when the untrained says the really wrong thing that lands you in court or in mediation due to an EEOC claim. I've seen it, and I bet you have too.

There is nothing wrong with including a variety of people from the organization in the interview process; however, anyone who speaks to prospective new hires should be trained in interviewing techniques and have a specific role in the interview process. At bare minimum, interviewers should be briefed on basic interviewing points and what can — and cannot be — asked in an interview.

HIRING SHIPWRECK #5
Lakeside Luxury Loss:
Flawed interviewing processes

Firms that maintain a basic interview strategy and ensure anyone who speaks with candidates is prepared with the knowledge to add value and avoid damage in the interview process consistently make better hires and maintain higher retention rates. This goes for small firms as well, even those with-out a full-time human resources manager. So much information is available on the subject there is no excuse for not being prepared. Many firms choose to take the train-the-trainer approach, where one or more people in the firm are trained in interviewing, as-sessment and selection techniques, then are responsible for training others in the firm and for maintaining interview and selection process integrity.

Each firm is unique, and based upon fac-tors such as geography, cross-collaboration needs, technical expertise, required industry experience, firm culture among others; there is an optimal process for each firm. Some companies choose to interview in groups to strive for efficiency and observe how the candidate(s) interact with one another and the interview team. Other organizations prefer individual interviews, often "ladder-ing" the process whereby candidates must pass through interviews with lower level managers before meeting with senior manag-ers. The intent is worthy (to make the best use of senior management's time); however, the process should be managed to avoid any of the Ten Hiring Mistakes as the candidate climbs the interview ladder.

The recent advances in audio/video technology provide an opportunity for firms to take a look at their historical interview process and refine it to achieve efficiency and interview depths that were heretofore not available. Using real-time, video-enabled online and mobile meeting tools, it is easy and inexpensive to replace the traditional initial phone screen interview with a face-to-face interview. The ability to see a candidate and his/her body language is exponentially better than just a voice call. Additionally, these platforms allow participants to join from anywhere in the world. One of our clients recently asked me to sit in on a vice-president level interview for a key position in her organization. The interview went well and it made little difference that we met via video conference with me attending from a Delta Sky Lounge in Atlanta, the candidate in Dallas, and senior managers from the client organization in Baltimore, Reston, and San Diego.

Another cautionary note on organization interviewing processes that must be shared is to beware of falling into the "more is better" mindset. For years, two of our clients had maintained an interview process wherein candidates (manager level and above) who had passed the initial phone screening phase were flown in for an immersion interview. The process consisted of a dinner the evening before the interviews, followed by candidate interviews with managers from all areas of the organization, often for 8 to 10 hours. The utilitarian intent of making the most of the day often resulted in exhausted candidates who were unsure who really made decisions in the organization. Worse yet, one company that had indicated the process was over and a decision on an offer would be made in short order, afterwards requested the candidate fly to two other cities to meet other senior members of the organization. For a C-level position this very well may be warranted. However, for general and mid-level positions this may be overkill. Twice in the past six months, good candidates opted out of consideration for the positions because they deemed the process excessive.

HIRING SHIPWRECK #6
Ski Chalet Shove: The favorite son (or daughter, nephew, etc.)

It is only fair to qualify this section by stating second generation family members and other relatives can work in the business, and often add great value. This is often achieved through a combination of being exposed to the family business from a young age and managing their integration into the business through a defined succession/integration plan — ideally after the incoming family member has worked outside of the family business for a period of time.

The loss of time and money and family fractures tied to nepotism are almost always linked to one of a few key mistakes, or a combination thereof:

The assumption from birth that a given family member will work in the business in a leadership position. In this scenario, often the only one happy about the assumption is he who made the assumption. The management-by-birth-right scenario often leaves many others disengaged, including other managers who have worked their way up the organization, other hardworking employees who chafe at the favoritism, and often the birthright family member. Imagine how it would feel for someone to have their career predetermined for them. This dysfunctional scenario has and will keep consultants in business for a long time, and has also resulted in some of the most expensive condo-sized losses we've seen!

Lack of clarity - Another mistake that begins with good intentions occurs when family members are brought in and told to learn the business. Depending upon the behavior style of the individual, the result is usually not much learning taking place or the bull in the china shop scenario, where the junior family member begins bossing people around, changing long standing policies without understanding the organization and severely damaging culture before the exit.

Lack of communication around the addition of any new manager can be damaging, and only more so when it is tied to the addition of a family member. Even when the senior and junior family members have a plan, it is often not communicated throughout the organization because they don't want to make waves or they simply assume everyone will understand the plan. This could not be further from the truth. We have worked with several firms where family members were brought into the organization without communication (even to senior staff) about the whys, whats, and hows of the position. Remember, most people listen to the radio station WIIFM — What's In It For Me? Not knowing the intent or strategic plan for the addition of one or more family members can be extremely deflating for others in the organization, resulting in passive aggression and political blockades toward the family member, departures of key employees as well as risers in the organization, and the ultimate failure of the hire.

HIRING SHIPWRECK #7
Hawaiian Hideaway
Hiccup: Groupthink

Groupthink is defined by the Merriam-Webster dictionary as "a pattern of thought characterized by self-deception, forced manufacture of consent, and conformity to group values and ethics." For the purposes of this book we define it as another condo-sized result of poor hiring tactics. Groupthink can be driven by a larger-than-life company leader who dominates his/her management team to the point of no dissension. We also find groupthink in organizations with a culture reticent to conflict, where speaking up is uncomfortable and generally avoided at all costs. As a result, hires are made that never should be.

HIRING SHIPWRECK #8
Countryside Cottage Crumble:
Rite of passage promotion

In my experience the second costliest hiring mistake after the Favorite Son is the Rite of Passage tragedy. This refers to the lack of discipline or tenacity in the hiring process, allowing an organization to promote an internal candidate beyond their level of capability. Most people are familiar with the phrase "a great salesman does not always make a good sales manager." This refers to the specific attributes required for highest and best use in a given job, including certain behaviors, motivators, competencies and natural talents (or acumen indicators). In the example highlighted in the phrase above, the attributes needed for a successful sales manager, things like managing others, coaching, leadership, conflict resolution, are vastly different from the attributes required for many sales positions, including things like tenacity, working independently.

Along these lines, too many organizations still make the assumption high performance in one position automatically correlates to high performance in another. Often the promotion is made to reward hard work, loyalty, and tenure. Sometimes the promotion is for political reasons, and other times we see these ill-fated promotions being made out of sheer laziness. The organization simply did not take the time to conduct a proper search for a better fitting candidate from outside of the organization.

When these promotions fail, they are expensive. Often signals of the mis-hire/ mis-promotion appear very shortly after the promotion, sometimes as early as days or weeks. And now the organization finds itself stuck. How do they unwind the promotion of a longtime and loyal employee? There are a variety of ways, almost all of which are expensive.

What can you do to mitigate your risk? When you think the internal employee is ready for the promotion, but are not com- pletely sure, one option is to promote to an interim. That is, make the promotion on an interim basis for 90 days, allowing for a much softer landing should it not work out, and also providing time to search outside the organization a bit more to create a back-up candidate pool, if necessary, to draw upon.

HIRING SHIPWRECK #9
Poolside Condo Plummet:
Weak candidate pool

In today's market and with today's technology, there is no excuse for an organization not to develop strong pools of candidates for individual positions, and to maintain pools of candidates for positions that require frequent hires due to growth, seasonality and other reasons.

Simply put, if you have a small pool of candidates, chances of being able to choose from two or three prime, A-player, candidates are slim. Often the only choice is from among a few B- or C-player candidates. Your organization deserves better; you deserve better! Too often are we brought in to fix a hiring tragedy that could have been avoided if the company had taken the time or deployed the resources to develop a stronger pool of candidates.

It should be noted, however, the methodology for sourcing candidates has changed dramatically in recent years. Newspaper classifieds are an expensive relic of the past, and even most job boards are a waste of time, often resulting in the Talent Pool

Paradox, which we will explore in more detail in Chapter 5.

For the purposes of this discussion, know there are efficient and cost-effective ways of building and maintaining strong candidate pools.

HIRING SHIPWRECK #10
River Ranch Renege:
Getting romanced or sold

Even I have been guilty of getting romanced and sold by a candidate. However, I pride myself on learning from my mistakes. My worst condo-equivalent failure in this area (over a decade ago) was the inspiration for my research into search and selection and the ultimate development of our award-wining process.

His name was Bryan and we interviewed him for an outside sales position when I was president of a 100-person organization in 2002. Attending the interview with me was a highly competent second-generation senior manager named John. John and I worked well together, leveraging one another's strengths to professionalize and grow a decades-old profitable family business. We opened new offices together, hired dozens of people together and were not hesitant to engage in healthy spirited debate when we did not agree on something. We really made a good team and were supported further by a solid management team. John and I interviewed Bryan over a casual lunch.

Bryan came from the industry, had worked for a worthy competitor and was not encumbered by a non-compete. He came recommended by a manufacturer's representative, and quite simply had us at "hello." Bryan was a salesperson and salespeople are often the best interviewees. Why? They are great at selling themselves! He said all the right things, knew our product lines, told funny jokes within acceptable bounds, talked about the customers he could bring over to our firm, and convinced us that $2 million in sales would be his minimum contribution. We let objectivity fly out the window, didn't get relevant references, and ultimately hired Bryan at a base salary higher than normal due to our confidence in his contribution to our company's top and bottom line. We were romanced; we were sold!

In less than a month we started to suspect we may have overestimated Bryan's level of product knowledge, depth of customer relationships, work ethic, and morals. It went from bad to worse and Bryan was gone within a few months, costing us a nice condo! The word that underscores the lesson from this is objectivity. Do not make hiring decisions solely on subjective information. Even when you like the candidate, force yourself to check the facts and follow an objective selection process. We will go into options for many levels of objectivity and checks and balances later in the book. In the meantime, remember to insist on objectivity to avoid being romanced or sold.

Once again, everyone who has been in business for any reasonable period of time has a hiring shipwreck tale to tell — but some scenarios are more common than others. In the next chapter we'll describe the most common shipwreck and explore the role this individual commonly plays in organizations. We'll also share how to identify these individuals and create plans for dealing with them before they cost the company more time, emotional energy and lost prosperity.

Doing a Shipmate a Favor

Patricia and I worked together in complementary departments for the same company. After separately leaving the company, we maintained a ten-year friendship and enjoyed similar career tracks in our respective fields. Although both of our careers advanced, hers did not go as planned financially and she found herself working in an unhealthy company/environment. Trying to help a friend, I hired her into an entry level, non-management position reporting directly to me. From my perspective, she could be autonomous, secure a higher salary, and begin a track in a different functional area in her same industry. From her perspective, I didn't give her enough support; I wasn't fully utilizing her skills, and owed her special exceptions because we were friends.

I realized a few months into the hire I had made a drastic mistake. She asked for a day off, I simply replied "I'll check the calendar," and was immediately met with a hostile declaration of "It's for my fertility treatments — and if you don't give me the day off, you'll be the reason why Ben and I don't have kids!" Over the

next year, her distress with me contin-
ued on many management decisions she
didn't agree with, and she openly ex-
pressed her dismay with me. Eventually, I
accepted a promotion with another com-
pany; Patricia felt abandoned. The expe-
rience ruined a ten-year friendship. We
barely spoke for years, and still exchange
only casual conversation when we cross
paths at professional conferences. From
this experience I learned the true mean-
ing of "right fit" when it comes to hiring
decisions!

CHAPTER 4

The Threefold Business Cost of Donnie

Several years ago, I was facilitating a board of directors' retreat for a very successful third-generation family business in northern California. Staying true to the region in which the business had operated for many years, the choice of Sonoma Valley for the retreat was natural. The setting was beautiful as the fall sun set on the vineyards and sparkled off the leaves of the grapevines, which to my surprise changed colors in the fall.

A few of the board members flew in and arrived throughout the afternoon, and all of the family members were on time for the night before board meeting dinner, all except for Donnie. Donnie was part of the third generation of owners who was part of the business by birthright; however, had not quite found his role, other than acting as the de facto life of the party. To ease the tension of the delay of dinner for 12, Donnie's father played the role of impromptu tour guide around the vineyard, even portioning out handfuls of the magical volcanic soil that gave the wine its unique character. As the 15-minute tour dragged to an hour, the 8 p.m. dinner became a 9 p.m. reservation. All of this was surely wearing on the folks who had traveled from the East Coast, whose internal clocks were three hours ahead, rounding on midnight.

Finally someone announced with positive affect, "Here comes Donnie!" and pointed to the convertible making its way up the vineyard lane and leaving a trail of Calistoga dust in its wake. What happened next is the reason the Donnie phenomenon deserves its own chapter. As Donnie positioned his new coupe safely away from the group, but close enough for everyone to get a good look at his new wheels of wealth, Donnie's father rushed over to the car and asserted, "What's with those license plates?" Donnie very proudly explained he had taken the initiative to order vanity tags that displayed the name of the family company — he was actually beaming as if he had sealed the deal for an attractive merger. Unfortunately, Donnie's father and chairman of the board saw things differently. While the hungry and tired board of directors stood uncomfortably by, Donnie's father yelled, "Are you crazy? Putting our company name on your license plates and a company vehicle?! The next time you back into another car outside of a bar or rear-end someone, which with your record will be in the next three weeks, they'll know exactly who you are! Dammit, son, you need to keep a lower profile until you get your act together!"

To his credit, Donnie was charming. He was surely talented in something; however, he just hadn't found his place in the family company. Herein lay the two reasons the Donnie phenomenon deserves its own chapter: 1) because the opportunity cost cuts both ways, and 2) because versions of Donnie exist (for a variety of reasons) in a large number of the companies and organizations we work with.

First, it is critical to emphasize the importance of the exponential opportunity cost in a Donnie situation. To frame the conversation, opportunity cost is defined as the "option foregone." For example, if I am an accountant paid by the hour and I take a vacation, my cost consists not only of the cost of the vacation, but also the cost of the money I would have made had I worked that week instead of going on vacation; hence, the opportunity cost.

In a Donnie scenario, the opportunity cost for the business is three-fold:

1. The hard costs of keeping Donnie on the payroll (salary, car, benefits, sometimes legal, etc.)

2. The cost foregone by not having a competent and fully productive team member in the seat that Donnie is occupying

3. The intangible cost of the drag on engagement of other good team members who are tired of putting up with or working for Donnie!

To be clear, Donnies come in all genders, shapes and sizes, a few of which follow:

Bloodline - As in our sad but true example of Donnie in the convertible, this scenario is being played out concurrently and undoubtedly thousands of times in firms of all sizes across the United States and beyond. While no one can fault the dream of a business owner to have his next generation add value to the business, the blind-eye scenario unfortunately is understandably a powerful drug that costs organizations time, talent and untold profits. Only the most astute and disciplined business owners seem to find the proper balance of love and fortitude to put Donnie in a position of his highest and best use, or exit him from the business in the greater interest of the business, family, and ultimately, succession and wealth.

Political - The lines are blurred a bit in this Donnie scenario as opposed to a scenario involving a direct family member. We see politically-appointed Donnies for a number of reasons: perhaps a friend of the boss is hired or a son/daughter of a friend of the boss is hired, or an organization hires someone from a customer or vendor in order to strengthen the relationship. In all cases, the reason for the hire is political or personal.

Legacy - The legacy Donnie is one of the toughest to resolve. The legacy Donnie refers to that loyal worker who has put in their blood, sweat and tears for years, often decades, and the business has simply moved to a pace faster than the legacy employee can keep up with. Take, for example, an architect who in addition to his regular duties managed the specification library. Over time the firm grew, as did the library, and managing the library became this Donnie's full time job. While he was the go-to guy for the resident architects and maintained wonderful relationships with the manufacturer's representatives, who visited regularly to demonstrate new products, this Donnie hadn't practiced architecture design in years. While he was a convenient resource for practicing designers, 95 percent of the information needed by the practicing designers was available online at the push of a button. In essence, this Donnie became obsolete. Again, this is one of the hardest scenarios — in this case a good person who has been rendered obsolete by technology and new practices. Typically strong in character and loyal team members, they unfortunately become a Donnie due to the opportunity cost identified above.

Tenure - Different from legacy, tenure refers to the Donnie who has simply been there so long that corporate conventional wisdom finds it difficult to confront the issue. We recently worked with a firm that had a finance manager who had been in her position for 24 years, was severely resistant to change and generally did not get along well with others.

The firm was experiencing challenges associated with the economic downturn and needed to tighten belts throughout. When we benchmarked the position, it became clear the finance manager was actually performing the much lesser role of a bookkeeper. To make matters worse, due to her tenure through annual pay raises and cost of living increases, this bookkeeper was making well into six figures. Add in six weeks' vacation due to her tenure, prime parking, and other fringe benefits, including box seats to the local baseball team (true story!), this well-tenured bookkeeper was costing the firm over $200,000 per year. Again, we must qualify the discussion here — by no means are we advocating replacing valuable employees with lower cost employees. We are simply illustrating the costly effects organizations find themselves in due to various Donnie scenarios.

Blackmail - Perhaps we should call it the "don't ask, don't tell" Donnie. Many firms find themselves in Donnie scenarios as a result of a situation or situations where Donnie has been exposed to financial, moral or otherwise compromising misdeeds of upper management and could potentially hold the trump card if push comes to shove. Thus, blackmail Donnie is left to graze in the company pasture. For all business executives and business owners and future business executives and business owners — DO NOT allow your company to be in this position, period. This is one Donnie who is almost never unwound without serious consequences, financial and otherwise.

Loyalty/Executive Mandate - For reasons sometimes hard to decipher, many Donnies exist due to executive mandate or otherwise sheer loyalty. Another extreme opportunity cost that is difficult to unwind, many executives and / or business owners develop a loyalty (often due to friendship that blurs into a friendly version of the Blackmail category) to one or more team members in the organization. No matter how inept and insubordinate this Donnie tends to be, the executive/owner just cannot find it in his or her heart to pull the trigger and make the change. The opportunity cost is often greater in this situation than the others, as Donnie is usually highly compensated, and the toxic situation continuously drives high-potential team members away.

In summary, understand the current state of your organization. If Donnie exists at any level it could be costing you hundreds of thousands of dollars, increased turnover, and lower productivity, engagement and profit. In this scenario you must make the change, albeit civilly and respectfully, in order to re-build and hire again — a better hire — one vetted through a proper selection process for the safety and success of the company in the future.

The First Mate Who Never Was

While on a college campus recruiting interns, a colleague and I were interviewing an adult student with a fairly long job history. She was an extrovert, easy to talk to and pleasant throughout the interview. She made great eye contact, appeared confident and was knowledgeable. There was no reason for my nagging sense she might be troublesome in the position, but after 24 years in hiring, my instincts and training are well-honed. When my less experienced partner disagreed, I dismissed my concerns and placed her résumé in the maybe pile.

As our recruiting progressed, several of the star candidates dropped out and we were left with this individual. We sent her résumé, along with those of two other candidates, to the hiring manager. She was chosen and accepted the internship. This is when things fell off course: She was late on her first day and claimed no one had told her what time to show up, despite evidence to the contrary. Then her background check came back with a fraud charge, which she claimed to have no knowledge of. She staged an emotional scene when it was discussed. As a result, we decided to withdraw the internship offer. She had only been employed three days.

Refusing to be deterred, the candidate called, cried, begged and pleaded to several different leaders throughout the company. She even called the customer service hotline. We caught her in several outright lies as she tried to convince us to rehire her. Since her background check was the reason for the termination, it was decided we would simply pay her for the length of the internship, which amounted to almost $9,000. This gave her no ability to claim any damages should she decide to proceed with litigation, which she threatened several times in her many phone calls to us.

Despite the upheaval, it was a good learning opportunity for my assistant and a great reminder to me to listen to my instincts, born from experience.

CHAPTER 5

The Talent Pool Paradox

With all of the downsizing and employee shake-ups during the Great Recession and the user-friendly internet tools at our fingertips, one would think it is now easier than ever to quickly and efficiently find the right talent to fill job openings, right? Well, yes and no. While most people think the above statement is correct, in reality it couldn't be further from the truth. In our recruitment and selection work with clients throughout the Americas and in discussions with business leaders from all over the world, we find ourselves regularly helping people understand the phenomena I call the Talent Pool Paradox.

The Talent Pool Paradox refers to the reality that the challenge of finding the right talent has increased exponentially over the past few years. Due to the convergence of three primary, yet vastly different forces, one must adopt a new paradigm in order to hire and retain good talent. If this paradigm is understood and the proper techniques are applied, forward-thinking organizations can actually leverage the Talent Pool Paradox in their favor.

The three forces converging to develop the Talent Pool Paradox are 1) social 2) economical and 3) technological. We will cover these individually shortly; for now let us begin by recalling how selection and hiring was (for the most part) done just a few years ago. Using the Traditional Model, when an organization needed to hire someone, it went something like this:

The business owner, executive, human resources manager or whoever was responsible for the hire would place a classified advertisement in local papers that typically included the job description along with other pertinent information. Depending upon the industry, specialty nature of the position or the position's seniority, ads were sometimes placed in industry publications or papers with a broader reach than the local papers. While the hiring manager waited for résumés to arrive by snail mail (and within the last decade by email), he or she would also network through word of mouth, be it with neighbors, the country club, or various professional organizations.

Over the next few weeks, résumés would arrive, the volume of which typically depended upon the desirability of the position as well as the local economy. The hiring manager would then screen, interview and eventually select a candidate, thus fulfilling the process. When the choice made was a hiring mistake, the process would be required again — and sometimes yet again.

THE TALENT POOL PARADOX

Over the past few years, social, economic and technological forces have converged in such way that the candidate pools developed from recruitment efforts are most often huge; much, much larger than historical talent pools. While this may seem like a positive result on the surface, when one dives into the pool, they quickly discover the paradox — that only a small percentage of the talent pool are decent candidates for the respective position!

See the forces converge:

The three forces contributing to the Talent Pool Paradox:

1. **Social** - Just a generation ago it was common and often expected that the company you joined for your first full-time job would be your career home. Most people would simply be promoted to their level or competence (in some cases incompetence) and stay with their respective company until they retired. When people did make career changes, it was usually to go out on their own or take a similar job for a competitor of their legacy company. No matter what the case for the change, hiring managers most often frowned upon "job-hoppers" and almost always viewed résumés with two or three company changes during a career with skepticism.

Time has changed things. Now it is highly uncommon for people to stay with the same company for their entire career, and changing jobs as a way to further one's career and professionally develop one's skill set is the norm. Many people attribute lack of company loyalty to the most recent generation. But my belief is that from Gen Xers forward, employees realize the significant percent-

"Now it is highly uncommon for people to stay with the same company for their entire career, and changing jobs as a way to further one's career and professionally develop one's skill set is the norm."

age of their waking hours are spent working, and they simply want to spend that time in the manner that either least sucks, or in the manner and for a company with which they can be fully engaged. This worker liberation boils down to two simple things:

a. Life's too short to be miserable at work, and
b. People will leave bad bosses.

The result is more people looking for jobs, be it actively or passively. To make the distinction, an active candidate is one who is actively engaging in a job search. Whether they are emailing résumés to any job that catches their eye or quietly searching job boards on weekends or while they work in the comfort and privacy of their own office, these candidates are actively looking. Passive candidates, on the other hand, are those who are either happy in their current role but open to better opportunities or those who are disengaged but sticking it out due to golden handcuffs (financially indentured servitude) or simply because they are too busy balancing work and life to actively search for a position. Our search team refers to this latter group as "perched," as in currently attached to a branch but could flap their wings and fly anytime.

In summary, the social changes in recent years and acceptance of people changing companies over the course of their career has resulted in more candidates in play at any given time.

2. **Economic** - The Great Recession, corporate downsizing and the shift to outsourcing and part-timing (often to avoid health care costs) has shifted the employment sand for millions over the past few years. The economic factor is likely a larger contributing factor to the Talent Pool Paradox than the social factor, and it has added to a tsunami wave effect in the

overall talent pool — not to mention how it has added to the stress levels in households throughout the United States and beyond.

3. **Technology** - Weighing in with larger amplitude than the economic factor is the third contributor to the Talent Pool Paradox: technology. Today's online access to job information is better than ever. What began a few years ago with sites like Monster and CareerBuilder has blossomed into innumerable networked resources.

The real result is an overcrowded pool with most candidates falling in the weak or are-you-kidding-me categories of consideration. While the hiring manager role (whether it is the business owner, human resources, or other) still differs based upon size and culture of the organization, the managers responsible for hiring often find themselves simply overwhelmed by the volume. This adds significantly to the chances of making a hiring mistake. What comes next varies depending upon the situation, but in most cases the hiring process does not go well.

First, like a large basket of laundry that needs folding, no one wants to begin the laborious process of starting to go through the tidal wave of cover letters and résumés. When the process is finally started, keeping track of the candidates and sorting them into some hierarchy is cumbersome and usually poorly done. The resulting delay often produces lost opportunities for good candidates (they lose interest or are snatched up elsewhere), as well as hiring mistakes on the part of the company. These mistakes are so ubiquitous we've been able to identify six common errors companies large and small, and positions from CEOs to entry-level, make.

The first common mistake we see is something we refer to as FIFI — or First-In, First-In. This means the first handful of résumés to hit the inbox gets the most attention. Imagine the lost opportunity to the company (and prospective good hire) of talent that never even gets to the proper consideration stage. In this scenario, timing is everything and candidates who simply submit at the wrong time are eliminated arbitrarily.

Another variation of this is LIFI, or Last-In, First-In. File this in the sad-but-true category; unfortunately we have witnessed this phenomenon far too often. The LIFI scenario refers to hiring managers who post an ad and set up an email to which candidates send their résumés. The inbox goes unattended for a week or two, simply filling as candidates email their information. At a time chosen by the hiring manager (or when he gets around to going through the résumés), he starts at the top of the inbox (last one to arrive, hence "last-in,") and goes down until he has a handful of candidates he feels are worthy of an interview. Imagine again the potential for poor job fit, hiring mistakes, and lost opportunity of the treasures left unattended in the inbox.

Another common mistake results in poor job fit. In other words, the overwhelming effect of the Talent Pool Paradox on many hiring managers results in selection of candidates poorly fitted for the job. This may seem contradictory, since with so many candidates from which to choose, chances should be higher of finding strongly fitted candidates. The reality is many time-starved hiring managers take a "stop the noise" approach and hire the first candidate from the large pool that meets their basic criteria.

"Despite the additional ways to exchange information and connect in today's world, finding good people remains a challenge."

A fourth error we refer to as Ill-will, and it is a newcomer to the hiring market. Due to the internet and the rise of social media, there are now plenty of outlets for employees and candidates who want to speak out about their employer, or in many cases, their former employer. Sites like glassdoor.com allow a sort of rating and review ability for employees to voice their opinion about companies for which they have worked — many opinions of which are not positive.

The final two mistakes are recruiter zero (or anemic value-add) and extreme in-house cost per hire. With recruiter zero, traditional recruiters simply open their virtual drawer of candidates and send candidates to hiring managers with the sole intent of filling the position as quickly as possible so the recruiter can get paid. This only adds to the chop and the depth of the Talent Pool Paradox, providing little or no value to the overall hiring process. Extreme in-house cost per hire involves those virtuous hiring managers who actually take the time to review each candidate, further process those who on the surface seem to be qualified, and rack up many hours on a laborious search and selection process. Implementing the process adds up to a tremendous expenditure of time and energy, resulting in a very high cost-per-hire rate. Despite the additional ways to exchange information and connect in today's world, finding good people remains a challenge. In fact, due to the Talent Pool Paradox, it has become more of a challenge, even for those with the best of intentions and a good hiring process. The Talent Pool Paradox poses new challenges for hiring managers and companies that have not been confronted on this scale before. This new reality calls for a new approach to hiring that avoids the pitfalls of a 21st century business world.

Poor Fit Nearly Capsizes Crew

As my firm grew, my partner and I recognized the need to build a collaborative team who were willing to accept added responsibilities and accountability. One of the team's first decisions was that our business had grown into two distinct entities with conflicting resource requirements. Based on that structure, we agreed to establish separate business units with managers responsible for the entire process of development through sales.

I hired a group business director whose experience included a stint at a multinational professional services company, managing and directing the sale of a midsized competitor, as well as various positions with competitive firms. We also hoped he would eventually organize a team of long-standing employees to purchase current ownership. Within months he let it be known current employees were not as smart as he was and that we should abandon our strategy for our largest business segment and pursue what he had seen work at different companies. Prior to his employment we discussed the benefit of disruptive change for the growth of the organization. Instead, he instituted disruption for personal gain.

Our culture is invaluable, our staff loyal, hardworking, and dedicated. It took nearly two years for me to release him for fear of offering him control but not granting responsibility to perform the position. Several of our key performers have since told me they were on the brink of abandoning the brutal workplace culture he established. I will never wait so long when I sense a bad fit because those were the two worst years of my career. He received bad legal advice after his dismissal and never signed the release fearing it would hinder his employment possibilities. He passed up well over $100,000 by doing so, yet had another job for a global competitor within three months.

CHAPTER 6

Attorneys, Used Car Salesmen and Recruiters

Several years ago I was president of a distribution company with a dozen locations from Boston to Virginia. The board of directors made the decision to open a location in the Carolinas. Not being familiar with the area, we engaged a local recruiter to help us staff the new office. Within just two or three days I received a UPS envelope with 40 or 50 résumés of candidates. Hoping to maintain an efficient process and get a feel for how the recruiter qualified the candidates, I called and asked the recruiter how he prioritized the dozens of candidates he sent me. Were they in order of recommendation, that is, were the ones on the top the most highly qualified? Also, how was he able to get so many candidates to us in such a short period of time? The pregnant pause on the other end of the line gave me cause to be concerned, and the ensuing conversation only added to my suspicion. The answer was that the recruiter simply made copies of résumés he had accumulated from prior searches as well as blind ads he had placed in prior months and years for jobs that did not actually exist, but rather for the purpose of simply building his résumé inventory! I immediately thought there must be a better way, and then filed that notion away for another time.

A few years later I was a C-level executive of a large national architectural firm. The economy was hot and so was the firm, resulting in constant demand for good design talent. The firm had a solid human resources manager and a long-standing relationship with a recruiter specializing in design professionals who gave the firm a special fixed rate for recruitment of architects. Charlotte, as we knew her, always seemed to have a steady stream of candidates at hand. We were generally pleased with the quality of candidates she sent our way, and we were an annual six-figure client for a number of years. Then came the Dallas Christmas party. It was December 2007 and about 50 employees and significant others were gathered at the fashionable Palomar Hotel north of downtown Dallas. The firm's president had just finished his remarks and my wife and I were speaking with a new employee. Ella was delightful, sharp and had a passion for the industry. I asked Ella how we came to hire her, and she mentioned that she had been referred by Charlotte, the recruiter. All seemed in order and for a moment I felt the investment we were making with Charlotte and her small specialty firm was a good one. Then came the question and answer that fueled the "there's got to be a better way" spark into a flame and real business. I asked Ella how she had connected to Charlotte. Her answer stunned me; Ella innocently stated, "Charlotte placed me at my previous firm last summer."

Fireworks went off in my head — Charlotte was churning! That is, similar to the way unscrupulous stockbrokers will buy and sell stocks in clients' accounts simply to generate the transaction fees, Charlotte was actually going back to the quality candidates she had placed at firms a few months prior, and poaching them in order to earn additional fees! I grabbed a beer and bar napkin and that very night began the business plan for a better way.

Unfortunately, sometimes attorneys, used car salesmen and recruiters are placed in the same pale light. The reality is there seem to be more bad recruiters than good recruiters. Many are motivated by their own self-interest instead of the best interests of their clients and their clients' companies. In addition, recruiters — as well as used car sales people and attorneys — suffer from a less-than-stellar public perception.

Because this book is about the importance of putting objectivity into the hiring process, we'll skip the discussion (and jokes) about attorneys and used car salesmen and focus on the value a professional and objective recruiter can bring to the search and selection process. First, let's explore why many people put recruiters in the necessary-evil box:

There seem to be more bad ones than good ones. The recruiting industry has low barriers to entry: low start-up costs and no requirement of an advanced degree or license. As such, many are attracted to the industry and drawn by the opportunity to make quick money. Like most professions, while money is often the result of the endeavor, when dealing with careers and livelihoods, money is the absolute last reason someone should become engaged in the industry. There is simply too much at stake.

Unfortunately, however, not everyone puts honor and ethics above ambition, and the result is a crowded field of recruiters, staffing agencies, and placement firms. Moreover, many people in the industry work "both sides of the desk." The side of the desk refers to which aspect of the recruiting process one is involved: the sales side or the fulfillment side. The sales side refers to client management: selling the process and communicating with the client. The fulfillment side refers to the actual search and selection process — the sourcing and screening of candidates for the position being filled. As an analogy, would you expect (or take the risk of) your real estate agent also being the person who does the title work when you buy or sell a house? No. You'd rather leave that to the experts.

The search and selection part of recruitment is both an art and a science. On rare occasions I have met people who have been in the industry a long time, focus on one specific industry for recruiting, take on one project at a time for a select group of clients, and are able to successfully work both sides of the desk. More often than not, however, the two-sided desk phenomenon seems to be a result of self-interest, specifically so the recruiter or firm in general can make more money.

Self-interest also appears in the recruiting industry, as some of the recruiting firms purport to specialize in a particular industry (banking, finance, sales, etc.). Certainly

"You are sure to find an ethical recruiter who will put you and your firm's interest above their own if you do some homework, ask some key questions, and of course, check references."

there are valid industry recruiting specialists out there, but be sure to do your homework and check references. Many of the self-proclaimed specialist firms choose the "specialist" angle simply so they can build one type of "inventory" (résumés) of candidates. This allows them to simply open their electronic file drawer for ready-made candidates at the first hint of a placement opportunity. Good for the recruiter, not necessarily good for the hiring company nor the candidate being placed.

The two stories at the beginning of this chapter are both stark illustrations of self-interest. In both cases the recruiter put individual interests above those of the clients or candidates. In our work with clients and hearing their past experiences, we have seen similar examples play out time and time again.

Take heart, however, that a few bad apples do not necessary spoil the entire barrel, and you are sure to find an ethical recruiter who will put you and your firm's interest above their own if you do some homework, ask some key questions, and of course, check references.

Suggested questions when considering engaging search and selection assistance are as follows:

- How long have you been in the recruitment or search and selection business?

- Why are you in this business? (Listen carefully to the answers.)

- Do you specialize in any specific industries or types of positions?

  - If so, why?

  - If not, why not?

- Do you screen candidates or just source them?

  - If they screen, then ask: What does the screening process entail?

  - Do you actually see the candidate before I do? (Note: with virtual meeting tools, smart phones and face-to-face meeting apps, there is no reason your recruiter should not always see a candidate's face before you do!)

  - Do you use assessments as part of your screening?

  - If so, what kind of assessments? (After you read Chapter 8, you'll have more insights into the additional questions you'll want to ask here.)

- Who in your firm does the actual sourcing of candidates?

- How do you source candidates?

- How many placements has your firm completed in the past two years?

"As the client, you always have a right to know the method and manner of recruitment."

- Of those, how many were successful? That is, the new hire lasted at least 12 months in the new position?

- Of those placed, how many were sourced specifically for the position (search engagement) and what percentage were placed from candidates already residing in your database?

- How do you charge for your services?

- What happens if the placement does not work out? What type of guarantee do you offer?

Armed with the answers to these questions, you will be in a much better position to select a search and selection professional who does not take shortcuts to get your position filled correctly, with a candidate well-suited for the job. In the process of asking these questions, you will also get a feel for how the recruiter approaches his or her work, which will provide insight into the candidates he or she will provide. Remember, as the client, you always have a right to know the method and manner of recruitment.

New Hire Shark Attack

The energetic, seemingly harmless COO with a résumé that touted a long list of embellished skill sets and attributes turned out to be a pit bull in sheep's clothing. After two managers quit within one week of her arrival and apparent bites, I knew I had a problem. Another week passed before discussing the brutal confrontations she was having with her reports. Yet, she was quick to tell me they loved her and I must enjoy drama. The drama ended at that point.

CHAPTER 7

How to Avoid the Talent Pool Paradox and Consistently Make Great Hiring Decisions

Up to this point we have spent a good deal of time covering the whys of hiring mistakes. People who know me will say focusing on negatives goes very much against my positive and optimistic nature. Covering the many reasons for hiring mistakes is imperative, however, due to the high cost of hiring mistakes, and the fact that most hiring mistakes are actually the result of more than one risk factor (for example, more than one bias, or a bias along with poor interviewing skills). The chance for a combination of risk factors exponentially increases the chance for a hiring mistake.

So how does one hire successfully, and is it possible to consistently make great hiring decisions? Of course! It comes down to two ingredients: 1) a system or process, and 2) inserting objectivity into that process. Hiring without a real process gives you odds similar to those at a blackjack table at a casino — a little less than 50 percent. That means you will win the hand (i.e. a successful hire) at best only once out of every two hands.

"Hiring without a real process gives you odds similar to those at a blackjack table at a casino — a little less than 50 percent."

Now refer back to the cost of a hiring mistake. You may remember the book "Bringing Down the House" by Ben Mezrich, or the movie "21," which was based on the book and starred Kevin Spacey. The book and movie were based on a true story of six MIT students who created a process using card counting and teamwork to turn the odds in their favor and consequently take Vegas for millions of dollars. The analogy rings true for the process we advocate for hiring — ideally without the melodrama in the book and movie! In summary, develop a process with the proper tools and you can greatly increase the odds of hiring success, and greatly reduce the risk of hiring mistakes.

The good news is you have the choice to implement a system yourself, retain a professional to assist, or develop a process that leverages a combination. While some nuances of the process will be unique to each organization depending upon its size and structure, the key components of an ideal search and selection process are as follows:

1. **Develop a clear understanding of the job for which you are hiring.** Fairly obvious, right? One would think. More often than not, however, we find that job searches are launched without a clear understanding of the actual key accountabilities of the job. In growing companies, if the position is new there is no precedent from which they can base the selection. Let's use the example of a director of operations position, the need for which often arises as a company adds employees, projects, and locations. The person responsible for hiring this position will often rely on job descriptions found on the internet or from peers who may or may not be from the same industry. It is just too easy to read a two- or three-page job description and say, "Yeah, that's what we need."

But wait, what will this new director of operations be responsible for? Project management? Staffing? Project profitability? Purchasing? Leasing? Contracts? You can see where this is going. A lot can fall under the title of director of operations, and this is true of almost any position. It is easy to leave the shore in search of talent without a clear picture of the destination. This happens so often. In the director of operations example, an ad is placed and the waves of the Talent Pool Paradox come crashing down! Even if the hiring manager is lucky enough to wade through the pool and find a candidate who seems to meet the criteria, without having a strong base of accountabilities for the position, the new hire will lack clarity and — worse — accountability. Odds of the new hire working out are less than 50 percent.

To get off to the right start toward a successful hire, begin with identifying the key accountabilities for the position. Many human resource professionals will cringe when they read this: scrap the job description (at least for this stage)! Get input from people who really know about the job. We call these people subject matter experts, or SMEs. An SME should be someone within one or two degrees of separation from the job; that is, they interact with the position on a daily or, at least, weekly basis. Simply, they know what responsibilities/accountabilities the job requires. Note: do not assume the team in human resources or the president or CEO naturally make good SMEs. While they may be involved in the process to some extent, these folks are often too distant from the position to add real SME value. Get input from your SMEs and identify three to five key accountabilities of the position.

The above will provide a strong foundation for the rest of the decisions you will make on your hiring journey. If you really want to kick it up a notch, however, learn more about job benchmarking: a process patented by our strategic partners at TTI Success Insights and used as the basis for all of the hiring for which we are retained. Job benchmarking not only employs a process for identifying the key accountabilities for a position, the process goes a few layers deeper by requiring the SMEs to rank (prioritize) the key accountabilities, then weigh those accountabilities (approximate percentage of time spent in each area) in order to develop a more laser-focused profile of prospective candidates.

2. **Identify the technical skills and other gate requirements for the position.** Once your key accountabilities are clear, identify the specific technical skills required for each accountability, developing a master technical requirement list for the position. This is an area often glossed over. By thinking through the technical skills associated with each key accountability, you have an almost foolproof way of developing a comprehensive list. These technical skills are considered "gate" requirements, as in "the candidate must possess these skills, certifications, etc. to get through the gate of initial consideration."

This is also the time to decide upon the degree requirements, years of experience, and other experiential assets you want your candidates to bring to the table. For each of these experiential requirements, decide

"To get off to the right start toward a successful hire, begin with identifying the key accountabilities for the position."

now whether they are hard (gate) requirements or simply desired assets.

Spending the proper time and putting the proper thought into these requirements and desired assets will serve you greatly when you begin sourcing candidates, and will also help mitigate your risk of drowning in the Talent Pool Paradox.

3. **Identify the competencies, attributes and soft skills required for the position.** This is a key area, as it gives you the opportunity to proactively identify the key attributes that will lead to great performance in the position and fit in well with your organization. Competencies, attributes and soft skills are somewhat relative in terms, and are best compared on a scale. Ideally they should be compared to what the job requires. Since

this is new for some folks, let us spend a little time on each term.

Competencies, attributes and soft skills refer to a certain level of mastery of various talents and are categorized in areas such as intellectual, personal, interpersonal, management and leadership. A good resource for competencies can be found in Dr. Bradley Smart's best-selling book "TopGrading." Other good resources are assessment results, which draw out the candidate's level of mastery in dozens of competencies, showing natural talents as well as potential blind spots. Our assessment suites of choice are those offered by TTI Success insights. (There's more to come on assessments in the next chapter.)

Developing your list of competencies, attributes and soft skills will help you avoid the risk of bias during the interview process. Here's how: if you develop your desired competencies ahead of time, you will be interviewing to draw out the level of competency match, uncovering if the candidate possesses an attribute or not. You will be prepared with the proper interview questions (Section 6 below), and thus weave objectivity throughout the interview process and decrease your risk of letting a bias slip in.

4. **Assign a project lead for the position.** Organizations on their game will have completed this task long ago; however, if you have not yet assigned a hiring project lead by this point, stop and do so. This should not take long at all; however, the choice is important and can be the difference between a hiring success and a hiring shipwreck.

Too often firms rely on human resources, an internal recruiter, or in the case of many small companies, the "go to" operations or administrative person for full responsibility when a hire is needed. This is generally the wrong thing to do. While HR and/or other administrative resources will surely play a role in the process, project ownership, responsibility and accountability needs to be placed on the supervisor most closely related to the hire. We hear clients complain ad nauseam about the poor quality of candidates being put in front of them by human resources or other internal resources. When the new hire blows up within the first 60 days, who do you think gets blamed? The same administrative component. Not only is this unfair, the lack of accountability is egregious.

Imagine an overwhelmed manager, who desperately needs more people on her team. She makes request after request and begs and nags to secure approval for the hire. Once she succeeds, she rushes to provide HR or the go-to administrative person her job order saying something akin to, "Fill this position, and by the way I need someone yesterday so find the perfect candidate ASAP!"

The problem is that even if HR takes all of the proper steps outlined above and below this step, the manager does not have a vested interest in the hire and no accountability if the new hire does not work out. Moreover, because this overwhelmed manager is busy with other things, she may or may not spend the necessary time on-boarding the new hire, further adding risk of a hiring mistake. We have heard countless stories of new hires who had been processed and hired through internal departments like HR, who arrive on their first day to an immediate supervisor who had no idea they were coming, no place for them to sit, and not a block of time cleared to properly on-board the new hire. Talk about first impressions! And this sad song is played over and over in companies of all sizes. Imagine how many misfires were counted as hiring mistakes when in reality it was a good hire, with flawed execution and no ownership. We call that dropping the baby.

The solution is that the direct supervisor is the natural project lead. This does not mean they are responsible for doing all of the steps; however, they are responsible for seeing that each step gets done, and staying involved throughout the process. We have seen sea changes in hiring performance and retention in clients who have implemented this ownership strategy. Ownership equals accountability, which leads to involvement, better decision-making, better hires, and fewer dropped babies.

5. **Develop a sourcing strategy for the position — and avoid the Talent Pool Paradox!** At this point you are almost ready to cast your candidate net and begin the sourcing process. This is also a pivot point for avoiding the Talent Pool Paradox. Since you have identified the key accountabilities, the competencies and soft skills and have an owner for the project, your task is to brainstorm about the best ways to source viable candidates for the position.

We recommend what we have coined, "the Wayne Gretzky approach" to sourcing. Years ago someone asked the all-time hockey icon how he always seemed to end up with or around the puck. Gretzky answered simply "I don't skate to the puck, I skate to where the puck is going." Ponder this for a moment. There is wisdom in Gretzky's statement and it can be applied to search and selection.

That is, rather than just placing the same job postings in the same online career sites or local papers or whatever the "same old process" is for your organization, put some proactive thought into how to get in front of the types of ideal candidates you have identified. Ideally, four or five "target channels," or places to hunt will provide you enough sourcing horsepower to yield a strong pool of candidates — and keep you from being tsunami-ed by the Talent Pool Paradox.

You can be as creative or as basic as necessary, the important thing is to focus on where your ideal candidates are hanging out. We have one client in Michigan that is a decades-old and well-respected structural engineering firm. A few years ago they went through the process of identifying three specific colleges that seemed to spawn graduates fitting their ideal profile. Then, they developed a multipoint and multi-touch plan to get in front of the best of those near graduates and develop credibility and positive stickiness over the course of a few strategic events. This process has yielded a steady stream of ideal candidates, the firm has hired steadily as it has grown, turnover is low and engagement is very high. Other clients focus on advertising on niche websites rather than large job boards, or strategically working certain trade associations. This is not rocket science, but there is some science involved, and the good news is anyone can do this!

6. **Develop competency-based interview questions for the position.** As mentioned previously, competency-based interviewing reduces the risk of allowing biases to overthrow the interview process. Additionally, pre-developed relevant questions are a huge help to most interviewers. Use experience based, open-ended questions relevant to the position and the ideal attributes you have identified in prior steps. The best teams develop several questions around each specific competency, which allows them to dive deep into areas of concern with a specific candidate, or with those the interviewer just wants to understand a little more. Multiple questions for each competency also allows the team to pre-plan who will ask which

questions, creating a smoother interview process overall and leaving candidates impressed with their experience interviewing with the team — a
win-win.

7. **Embark on sourcing, stay disciplined, review, adjust.** Once you
launch your search and begin sourcing, it is important to stay disciplined.
People may hear you are searching
and say "try this" or "try that." Additionally, you may have colleagues who
see you are hiring and will want to
throw a friend's name into the
hat. This is OK, so long as you bring
the referred friend in through the
same channel and apply the same
vetting process as other candidates;
otherwise you've just fallen victim to
peer bias.

It is fine to develop a plan B; however,
it is imperative you give your plan the
run it deserves. Otherwise you have
no way of judging the success of your
original plan. The project lead should
monitor candidate flow regularly and
at least weekly check with the others
on the search team and discuss progress. Depending upon candidate flow

after a week or two, you may need to adjust your strategy. This fine tuning is OK as opposed to haphazardly letting outside influences take over the process.

8. **Assess and screen candidates.** We will go into assessments in depth in the next chapter. For the purposes of developing and executing a high performance hiring process, **you should use assessments proper for the position being hired.** Depending upon your resources you may choose to assess only those candidates who pass the first gate check, or even those who are phone-screened. Find a good balance between information and cost that works for your organization. However, do not skimp on this step.

9. **Develop a pool of prime candidates.** Prime candidates are considered those who not only pass the initial gate checks and look good based upon their assessments, but those who somehow stand out through the initial process to the point where you feel like you have a fairly good chance of success if you were to hire any one

of these candidates. We recommend the project lead have a second set of objective eyes review the potential prime candidate pool as a bias check.

Your prime candidate pool should only be a handful — we recommend three to five but have submitted pools of up to seven when we had a large pool of simply terrific and well-fitting candidates. The intention is you will deep-dive into the prime candidate pool (more on that below) and ultimately make a hiring decision from one of these candidates. It should be noted, however, that culling the candidate list from 20 or more candidates to three to five can be difficult, and biases often creep in by way of lobbying from within the hiring organization. It is critical the project lead remains balanced and objective throughout this step — and it's his or her responsibility to decide upon the final prime candidate pool. This is accountability and ownership in action!

10. **Dive deeply into the prime pool.**
    Now that you have your pool of prime candidates identified, the real work begins. The specifics of deep-dive

are different for each firm depending upon its size; however, the objective is the same: to choose the candidate best fit for the position.

At this stage many firms choose to bring candidates in (separately or sometimes in groups) for a "day in the life," often rotating the prime candidates through one-to-one and group interviews, working their way up the management ranks and ultimately ending with the most senior managers. One of our favorite clients in Hunt Valley, Maryland, executes this portion with precision, starting interviews with lower management ranks and working up throughout the day. At any point along the way, if the interviewing manager feels the candidate will not work out well in the organization, he has veto authority and the interview process is ended and managers at upper levels are spared the time.

Incidentally, never bring a prime candidate in prior to some type of face-to-face interview. The quality of collaborative technology, ease of use and cost (often free!) leaves no reason to bring a candidate in sight unseen. Important note: this is not a beauty pageant; the reason for some type of face-to-face interview prior to the deep dive is to allow for more comprehensive communication. Studies have shown words make up only about 7 percent of total communication, and tone adds another 38 percent or so. Body language, whether it be from virtual meeting online or in person, essentially doubles the communication you receive from your candidates and that which they receive from you. So before you buy plane tickets and fly Ms. Prime Candidate in, have a visual, for goodness' sake!

11. **Conduct final due diligence.** After your in-depth dive, you will often have a candidate who clearly stands out among the rest. "We want that person!" is what we often hear. This is great, but please allow a bit of prudence that may save you time, embarrassment, and of course, big dollars.

Final due diligence includes reference checks, background check, and generally everything you can do to verify your intended hire is indeed the superstar you make them out to be. Based on the final due diligence you can be confident you have done everything you can to mitigate risk before your offer. In other words, should less than stellar information be received, you still will have the opportunity to walk away before you go to the W2 altar. If you make the decision to make an offer even after you receive some flags, at least you had fair warning and can put the proper controls in place to mitigate the risk of the same flag derailing your objectives and/or hurting your organization.

It should be noted there are information and background constraints at both federal and state levels, so do yourself a favor and outsource this relatively inexpensive, albeit priceless, task.

One more helpful hint: since you are going through the process of engaging background and reference checks, even if you have a clear winning prime candidate, perform the checks on your top three or four candidates, just in case your offer and subsequent negotiations to and with your number one candidate fall through (this could equate to a huge time-saver).

12. **Make a proper offer.** This is another area where savvy hiring firms leverage the task and lesser hiring managers lose the opportunity to develop a real relationship with their intended hire. Rather than looking at the offer as the final box to check off before the candidate accepts, view this task as an opportunity to put your best foot forward and communicate at an almost intimate level with your intended hire.

Think about it — everyone has heard the adage "the only thing worse than asking someone what they make is telling someone what you make." Salary discussions are simply taboo, something usually only discussed with spouses, mentors and the closest of friends. As a retained recruiter, time and time again, our clients expect us to make and negotiate the offer. We respectfully decline. The offer gives the hiring manager — ideally the project lead who should also be the direct supervisor of the new hire, the opportunity to talk at that intimate level. Granted, while the discussion is professional and often accompanied by a formal letter, the opportunity exists to develop trust through a personal shared conversation. Moreover, if your intended hire has any issues with any components of the package, you can resolve them right then and there rather than going through the uncomfortable and mind-numbing back and forth of an intermediary, be it human resources or an internal or external recruiter.

13. **Conduct proper onboarding.**
Onboarding is the last critical task in the hiring process, and unfortunately it is quite often overlooked. For the purposes of this discussion, we will assume the standard required new hire paperwork is taken care of through normal administrative channels. The onboarding responsibility of the project lead includes tactical and strategic orientation with the firm, proper introductions throughout the organization, and a meeting of the minds around the key accountabilities of the position, including specific expectations over the first few months.

In our recruitment practice, since we have established the key accountabilities and assessed any candidate who is ultimately hired, we develop a gap report (i.e. the gaps between ideal attributes and the candidate's natural talents) that allows us to pinpoint specific areas for professional development.

This tactic provides two components everyone wishes for but few achieve during the onboarding process: 1) clarity around the position and 2) accountability. These are worth repeating: clarity and accountability. Who could ask for more when bringing on a new team member, especially at the $100,000-plus level?

Through our work in recruitment, coaching, and emergency repairs of tragic hiring mistakes, we have found that historically, there is an inverse correlation to clarity/accountability and salary. That is, the higher the salary, the lower level of clarity and accountability.

"In most failed high-level hires, the problem lies in the fact that neither clarity nor accountability was established from the outset, and the executive was left to figure it out for himself or herself."

How can this be? The answer seems to be a combination of the lack of following a deliberate process as described above, and the "untouchable" that surrounds high-level executives as they enter an organization. For all but the most astute, confident and forthright managers, most folks tend to tread lightly (make that tiptoe) around high-level new hires. It is somewhat understandable. If the firm thought well enough to hire this big shot with the big title and salary, we should give that person free reign and general benefit of the doubt as they "find their way."

Wake up! There are real money, careers, and business objectives at risk here. In most failed high-level hires, the problem lies in the fact that neither clarity nor accountability was established from the outset, and the executive was left to "figure it out for himself or herself," resulting in frustration on the part of the new hire as well as the organization, another notch on the résumé belt 90 days later, and launching of yet another executive search.

14. **Schedule regular check-ins**. No matter what the level in the hierarchy of the firm, the project lead must conduct thorough check-ins at minimum every 30 days. Many managers prefer weekly one-on-ones, either in person or via web meeting, and this is even better. So no matter what your specific recipe for feedback loop is, the point to remember is the initial ramp up period is critical.

Consider a fishing boat leaving the dock for hunting grounds 70 miles offshore. The captain knows where the fish are — 70 miles offshore. He has all the data (key accountabilities)

and current fishing reports (assessments); he simply needs to motor
out to where the fish are (90-day
objectives).

While he might leave the dock with
coordinates set (onboarding), if the
captain doesn't regularly check the
boat's progress toward its destination
and adjust course as necessary (the
check-ins and feedback loop), even
if the boat is initially off course by
only 2 degrees, by the time he gets
70 miles out, the boat will be far from
the intended destination and he will
come back empty-handed (no results)
and sometimes even run out of gas
trying to find the elusive school of fish
(the tragic hiring mistake).

15. **Plan a 90-day review.** The final step
    to maximize chances of hiring suc-
    cess (no matter what the level of hire)
    is to conduct a formal 90-day review,
    ideally from a 360-degree basis. With
    the exception of a few rare stinky fish
    polluting the fishing grounds, the
    overwhelming majority of new hires,
    employees, and team members want
    to do a good job!

"Mapping your way through these waters is all in the details of your journey. Will it involve an investment of time and money? Yes. Will it be worth it in the end? Absolutely."

The 90-day review is more of a formal check-in to measure how the new hire is doing against established objectives and professional development plans. Moreover, it provides the opportunity for the settled-in employee to contribute valuable feedback based upon their experience in the organization to date, and the value they bring from their prior experience, be it from academia if they are a recent grad, or from the fishing grounds of the business pools in which they have been a part of over the years.

The difference between hiring and hiring successfully is the difference between sailing straight into a perfect storm and winning the America's Cup. Mapping your way through these waters is all in the details of your journey. Will it involve an investment of time and money? Yes. Will it be worth it in the end? Absolutely. As the captain of your vessel heading into stormy remote waters, what would you pay to avoid a shipwreck?

Emotions Lure Hiring Off-Course

A landscaping company was struggling to build a strong management team to be positioned for an aggressive growth strategy and overall recruitment and retention of key employees.

A formal selection process was implemented in order to increase successful hires and mitigate risk of bad hires. Each qualified candidate was fully vetted, resulting in a report concluded with a recommendation to hire, not hire or to hire with conditions.

On several occasions the COO, who was very emotionally driven, would "fall in love" with a candidate and question the validity of the process. With one particular candidate applying for a field manager position, the report was lengthier than usual and the final recommendation was a resounding "do not hire." This particular applicant, however, connected with the COO, who then took it upon herself to rewrite the screening report, allowing the candidate to pass with flying colors and be hired.

The COO placed this project manager on one of the company's high profile jobs. Within six months there were substantial internal concerns, and an external inquiry from local police. The company was unfortunately forced to terminate the field manager and hire a security firm to accompany the process.

CHAPTER 8

Are All Assessments Created Equal?

As discussed in Chapter 6, the proper use of assessments in the hiring process can significantly increase your chances of making good hires and correspondingly decrease your chances of making a hiring mistake. Assessments are extremely useful in professional development as well. A common challenge for managers, however, lies in the decision of which individual assessment or assessment suite to use. The market is flooded with choices, with literally hundreds of assessments from which business owners, coaches and managers can choose. Run a quick web search and you will see what I mean. But not all assessments are created equal — not by a long shot. Further complicating matters is the ease of graphic, web and online survey publishing, which allows almost anyone to create a report that looks good. This makes the amateur, non-research based assessment hard to differentiate from the validated, researched, legally sound and effective assessments out there. Choosing the proper assessment, however, is critical due to the stakes at hand.

"But not all assessments are created equal — not by a long shot."

In addition to the costs that accompany hiring mistakes, the improper use of assessments in organizations can add to legal exposure, which is the last thing you need when trying to hire. The intent of this chapter is to shed a little light on how to select an assessment that is reliable and safe, and offer some discerning questions helpful in deciding which tool to use for your particular organization.

First, let us define assessment as it pertains to the discussion of this book. Like many things, it is easier to describe what the assessment is not. For our purposes, the use of assessments to assist in the search and selection process, we will not cover technical assessments, which typically measure certain skill sets such as mathematical ability or technical competencies. While these types of assessments are common in many companies, they are also very specific to each particular company and used on their own or often in conjunction with the assessments we recommend to assist in the interview and selection process.

Second, we want to be crystal clear and emphatic that assessments should never be the stand-alone decision factor of whether someone is hired or not. There are simply too many other factors that go into a hiring decision. We view the use of assessments as an added tool in the hiring toolkit, which give us deeper insight into a candidate, including behavioral and communication style, natural motivators, competencies and natural talents. In this sense, the assessments we prefer really enable us to hire the total person and are unique in that they examine so many different aspects of candidates. In circumstances where a job benchmark has been completed for the position, assessments also provide a platform that allows for comparison between what the candidate naturally brings to the table and the optimal attributes identified for the position in the course of the job benchmark.

In our experience with firms throughout North America, we have found the use of certain types (or brands) of assessments seem to be concentrated in different parts of the country, while others are more global in nature. In areas of concentration, the choice of which assessment to use seems to be highly influenced by trusted advisors of those using the assessments. For example, leaders of executive peer groups often assess their members — and with good reason — to assist with peer advisory and executive coaching. As a result, many of the executives carry forward those assessments into their respective firms.

This tool can be a very good thing — provided the assessments are appropriate for the firm and the level of employees upon which they are used. Moreover, for assessments to be of optimal value they must be administered by a trained professional, ideally certified in interpreting and in professional development with the specific tool used. Like a caulk gun, assessments in the hands of the untrained can yield very messy results! Lastly, the most important element of the assessment used is its validity. Validity is one of pillars that make up the ideal assessment lighthouse.

The three aspects of an ideal assessment are as follows:

1. **Consistency** (aka reliability) - Consistency refers to how reliable — or repeatable — the results are. For example, if I take an assessment this year, then take the same assessment next year or the year after, all things being relatively equal, my results should be very similar to the time I first took the assessment. As an example, if I am in a fishing tournament and weigh a fish on the boat, place the fish into a live box, then weigh the same fish once we reach the judges

at the dock, the dock scale should give me the same result. (Note: This assumes we are an honorable fishing team and do not stuff the fish with ice or lead weights on the way to the dock). Hence, the scale is reliable or consistent because we are receiving the same reading from the scale both times.

In the assessment world, you will often see websites boasting consistency rates or reliability rates of 90 percent and above. This is a terrific rate, but it really should be expected in order for the assessment to offer any degree of reliability. Would you want to use an assessment that was 50 percent reliable? That would mean half the time, the assessment is inaccurate! Another factor to consider when you see these claims is how these percentages are established. Has an independent group validated the assessment? Are the percentages the result of in-depth research? Do these rates refer to just one assessment? Furthermore, does the assessment company possess just one assessment they use for all needs: selection, development, retention? Or do they have customized assessments,

"Do not be hesitant to ask good questions, and then pay attention to the specificity of the answer."

all of which have been validated, for different needs? What happens to the accuracy rate when the assessments are combined? Consistency, breadth and quality of the assessment all need to be considered. All assessments worth their salt should be reliable; however, these two following factors are arguably more important than consistency.

2. **Validity** - Validity refers to whether the results are actually correct. Simply put, is the measurement we are receiving giving us the correct reading for what we are trying to measure? Does the assessment you are considering have construct validity: meaning does the assessment as a whole measure what it says it does? In the fish example, just because the scales give me the same reading when I measure the fish at different times, if the scales are reading the incorrect

weight, it is not a useful tool at all, is it? There are other types of validity that any sound assessment company should also be validating — namely content validity, if the assessment questions match what is being tested, and criterion validity, how each assessment correlates to actual behavior in the real world. Good assessments are both consistent and of high validity.

Clients and seminar participants often ask how assessment companies validate their assessments. This is a good question, and one that we recommend you ask anyone providing (or trying to provide) assessment tools to you and your organization. The answers to questions about validation seem to vary as widely as the types of assessments themselves. But these are questions the assessment company should have ready and detailed answers for and supportive materials and outside resources to support. Do not be hesitant to ask good questions, and then pay attention to the specificity of the answer. (A list of assessment validation questions is provided at the end of the book.) If the representative seems shocked or ill-prepared, this is a definite warning sign. If the validation does not include an outside statistician, accounting firm or journal publication, be wary. Feel free to ask to see the company's validation studies before you adopt a new assessment tool into your organization. Similarly, if this chapter inspires you to go back and ask about validation of a tool already being used in your organization, then this discussion has served that intent as well.

Best-in-class assessment companies undergo significant time, effort and investment in their validation process because the research and the application of the tools developed are at the very core of why they do what they do. The best example I can think of is TTI Success Insights (TTI) based in Scottsdale, AZ. Chairman Bill Bonnstetter and his team have been creating and continuously improving their reports for over 30 years. All of TTI's assessments undergo a construct validity study. First, TTI engages outside statisticians to avoid the risk of in-house bias. The independent statisticians run the Cronbach alpha

"Highly effective assessments are a powerful tool to have aboard on your hiring journey."

to identify the level of consistency and validity. The validity study then uses the single-factor model on every single line of assessment, as well as the group as a whole. TTI then runs its own adverse impact studies, which are described in more detail below. Once TTI has run its own adverse impact study, it has the users of respective assessments run adverse impact in their respective organizations as well. Lastly, peer-reviewed articles are sought and encouraged, used as a cross-check of outside resources, which further validates TTI's validation and the outside statistician's initial research.

3. **Adverse impact** - Adverse impact can get complicated rather quickly; however the premise is this: it is illegal for hiring practices to discriminate against any protected class. Adverse impact studies prove or dis-

prove whether a certain hiring practice (or for the context of our current topic — assessments) discriminate. The federal government, particularly the Equal Employment Opportunity Commission (EEOC) and the Office of Federal Contract Compliance Programs (OFCCP) have invested heavily in adverse impact in recent years, especially in instances where failure to hire was the focus.

Using tools supported by adverse impact studies is extremely important for two reasons: 1) the potential legal exposure for non-compliant tools or hiring practices and more importantly 2) it is simply the right thing to do!

In summary, your ideal assessment should be supported by all three legs of the stool: **consistency, validity** and **adverse impact studies.**

Highly effective assessments are a powerful tool to have aboard on your hiring journey. Given the high quality, validated and legally sound assessments now available, there are more reasons to use them than not. Assessments, at their best, provide deep insight into the candidate and allow for points of departure and further discussion during your hiring process, as well as a good sense at the outset of what — and how — this individual will bring into your business.

Captain's Haste
Causes Major Wreck

A pharmaceutical company often has the need to fill highly skilled positions that require a specific niche set of skills which only a handful of people possess. To ensure we weren't settling for a candidate because they "fit the bill," we created a panel interview process consisting of an all-day interview and involving members of the executive team and key members within the department that was hiring. Upon completion of the interview the team would meet to discuss the candidate and make a recommendation to either move forward, move forward with qualifications or do not move forward. Move forward with qualifications meant the candidate would come back for a second interview for a deeper dive into any areas of concern or clarification.

One position was open for several months due to the specific technical skills it required. We found a candidate who met all the criteria and brought him in. Some of the interviewers voiced concerns about the integrity of the candidate based upon his responses to questions. The COO wanted this position filled, liked the candidate and decided to circumvent our standard process and hire the candidate.

The candidate was hired and shortly thereafter two issues arose. One was immediate, whereby his lack of credibility blocked buy-in from his peers and direct reports, which presented significant roadblocks in his ability to be successful in the role. The second unfolded over time and surrounded the integrity that was questioned during the interview process. This person missed deadlines, overpromised and under delivered, skipped meetings, and was often MIA. He took vacations at crucial times in the business when his involvement was critical and disrupted or blocked forward movement in a number of other ways.

The organization was hampered for almost a full year by this cultural misfit until ultimately the candidate was terminated and the search was restarted a full year later.

CHAPTER 9

Bringing it All Together: Charting Your Course Toward Blue Water

Over the last several chapters we have covered a good deal of territory, including but not limited to:

- Identifying the common (and not so common) hiring mistakes often made, and the reasons for many of those mistakes

- Identifying our roles in many of those scenarios

- Quantifying the costs of hiring mistakes

- Illustrating the challenges of recruiting in today's frenetically paced and hyper-connected world

- Putting more objectivity into the hiring process

- Identifying and sharing several tools to add objectivity and structure to the hiring process

- Shining light into the world of recruitment, search and selection

- Providing specific tools, questions and other considerations for you to significantly upgrade your recruitment and hiring process.

Now it is time for you to chart your course for how you and your organization will improve the way you approach hiring, whether you outsource the effort, manage it in-house, or employ an extremely effective hybrid model.

You must first identify the processes and systems that work best for your organization and situation. Like the great captains of huge sailing ships, enlist the assistance of a tugboat or bay pilot (a local expert) to get you out of the channel and into the open ocean. Many will argue, in fact, that the tools at our fingertips today are so helpful in stacking the deck in our favor — mitigating hiring risks and keeping us away from hiring shipwrecks — that it is downright irresponsible for a professional involved in selection, hiring and on-boarding not to put these tools to use.

Lastly, let us never forget the human side to hiring and the art of the selection process. Remember the assessments and other tools we use are barometers, not thermometers. That is, while the information gleaned from job benchmarking, assessment tools and a structured selection process will exponentially increase the chances of your hiring success and strong retention rates, never ignore a strong gut feel. To borrow a phrase from assessment patriarch Bill Bonnstetter, chairman of TTI Success Insights, "balance the head with the heart."

I sincerely hope you found this book helpful and wish you clear sailing in all your future hiring journeys!

ACKNOWLEDGEMENTS

Sincere thanks to Richard Sien for your incredible efforts in our pursuit of raising the bar of search and selection, and for your support with this project.

I also thank the anonymous contributors who shared their disaster stories, without which this book would be impossible.

Special thanks and recognition goes to Emily Soccorsy-Heetland, whose editing and project coordination made this book possible, and whose attitude and energy made it fun.

Acknowledgements

ABOUT THE AUTHOR

Mark Debinski is founder and president of Bluewater Advisory and managing director of its award-winning recruitment division, Bluewater Search, where he and his team provide leadership and organizational development, recruitment and succession planning services to clients across the United States. Prior to launching Bluewater, Mark worked in a variety of executive positions in the construction, logistics and design industry.

Debinski holds a Bachelor of Science degree from University of Maryland Baltimore County, and was awarded an Executive Masters of Business Administration degree with Beta Gamma Sigma honors from Loyola University Maryland. He is certified by TTI Success insights at the highest achievable levels, including Stages of Growth, TriMetrix HD, DNA, Motivators and Behaviors.

Debinski resides in Eldersburg, Maryland where he and his lovely wife Janet are blessed with two wonderful daughters and family dog, Sally. His hobbies include running, golf and saltwater fishing. Mark also proudly serves on non-profit boards of directors and is an advocate for the elderly.

Reach Mark at
mdebinski@bluewateradvisory.com
or learn more about Bluewater's
resources and services at
www.bluewateradvisory.com,
www.bluewatersearch.com
or 877-543-0525.

QUESTIONS TO ASK YOUR ASSESSMENT PROVIDER

Provided below is a list of questions from which to draw when discussing assessment validity with your assessment provider. Whether you are thinking of utilizing assessments for the first time, or have been using assessments for quite a while and want to now take a deeper look at the tool you are using, these questions should help provide some key information.

- Tell me about the assessment's consistency rating.

  - How often, on average, do you recommend assessing employees?

  - What do I do if we reassess a team member and find very different results?

- Tell me about the assessment's validity rating.

- Has a third-party validity study been completed?

  - When was it validated?

  - Do you regularly have the assessment re-validated as new versions are developed?

  - Can you provide me a copy of the validity study if I request it?

- What type of work has been done on the assessment regarding Adverse Impact?

  - Has there been a study? If so, what did it show? If not, why not?

  - Can you provide me a copy of the study if I request it?

- How has the assessment been improved in recent months or over the past two years?

  - Note: Good assessment providers are continuously researching and testing improvements, and should be rolling out refinements fairly regularly.

- How is the assessment delivered? Via paper, online or other?

  - How long does it take to get the results?

  - Does the participant taking the assessment automatically receive their results? Do they have to? For example, if I am using the assessments for hiring I might not want all of the candidates to receive their reports.

  - What are my customization options for the assessments?

- Where do I buy them? Can I buy them directly or do I purchase them through a consultant or third-party provider?

  - Why is the sales channel this way?

  - Are other people involved in the sales and delivery of the assessments and reports certified in the reports, or can anyone sell them?

  - How does this benefit me?

  - Can I buy a large block of assessments at one time to achieve a lower price per assessment?

- Why are you recommending this specific assessment?

- What other services do you offer along with the assessments that might help my organization?

- How do you, the assessment provider, stay current and continually improve your knowledge in the subject matter?

- Can I take a sample assessment?

- What are my customization options for the assessments?

- Can I put my company's logo on the report?

  - Are their benefits or possibly risks by doing so?

  - Can I rearrange the order of the information assembled in the report? How?

- May I speak with someone who uses this assessment regularly?

Of course, add any other questions pertinent to your specific situation. And remember two things:

1. If you are not getting straight answers, it likely is cause for concern.

2. Many assessment providers and consultants offer multiple assessments and even multiple suites of assessments. Ideally you should ask many of these questions about each specific assessment you are considering.

ACCOUNTABILITY & CAPACITY KEY

Accountability for Others: A willingness to take responsibility for the actions of other people.

Attention to Detail: The ability to pay attention to the specific elements, facets or parts of a situation or work assignment.

Attitude Toward Others: The general capacity one has for relating with other people.

Balanced Decision Making: The ability to make consistently sound and timely decisions in one's personal and professional life.

Conceptual Thinking: The ability to mentally envision comprehensive, long-range plans or goals and to identify, evaluate and allocate necessary resources.

Concrete Organization: The capacity to understand essential factors of a situation and bring together all necessary resources.

Conflict Management: The ability to resolve different points of view constructively.

Consistency and Reliability: The capacity to regularly and dependably engage in and complete tasks or processes.

Continuous Learning: The ability to take personal responsibility and action toward learning and implementing new ideas, methods and technologies.

Conveying Role Value: The capacity to communicate and promote the value and importance of one's role.

Correcting Others: The ability to objectively address the errors, omissions and/or poor results of other people.

Customer Focus: A commitment to customer satisfaction.

Decision Making: The ability to analyze all aspects of a situation to gain thorough insight to make decisions.

Developing Others: The desire to help others expand their talents and potential.

Diplomacy and Tact: The ability to treat others fairly, regardless of personal biases or beliefs.

Emotional Control: The ability to appear to be rational and in-control when facing problems or crises.

Empathetic Outlook: The capacity to perceive and understand the individuality in others.

Enjoyment of the Job: A measure of a person's attitude toward their current job or career.

Evaluating Others: The capacity to objectively assess or measure the abilities and performance of other people.

Evaluating What is Said: The capacity to objectively listen, understand and accurately interpret what someone else is saying.

Flexibility: The ability to readily modify, respond to and integrate change with minimal personal resistance.

Following Directions: The capacity to hear, understand and follow instructions.

Freedom from Prejudices: The ability to maintain objectivity when relating to other people.

Gaining Commitment: The ability to get support and "buy-in" from others for a specific goal or set of goals.

Goal Achievement: The ability to identify and prioritize activities that lead to a goal.

Handling Rejection: The capacity to exhibit persistence and strong will in the face of objections.

Handling Stress: The ability to maintain composure and internal strength when coping with external and internal pressures.

Influencing Others: The ability to personally affect others' actions, decisions, opinions or thinking.

Initiative: The compelling desire to get into the flow of work in order to accomplish the vision and complete the goal.

Integrative Ability: The capacity to see different components of a situation and tie them together to see the situation as a whole.

Internal Self Control: The ability to remain in conscious command of one's internal emotions when confronted with difficult circumstances and to respond rationally.

Interpersonal Skills: The ability to interact with others in a positive manner.

Intuitive Decision Making: The capacity to make decisions by looking at the most essential elements and without all the facts or data.

Job Ethic: The capacity to fulfill the professional responsibilities with a strong sense of moral duty and obligation they have been given.

Leading Others: The capacity to organize others in such a way that inspires trust and motivates people toward a common goal.

Long-Range Planning: The capacity to see the big picture and long-term goals and to forge clear, realistic plans to accomplish the desired results.

Material Possessions: An indicator of the desire to possess objects of high monetary value or importance.

Meeting Standards: The ability to perform work according to precise specifications.

Monitoring Others: The capacity to effectively oversee work done and decisions made by an individual or a team.

Objective Listening: The ability to listen to many points of view without bias.

Persistence: The capacity to steadily pursue any project or goal that a person is committed to in spite of difficulty, opposition or discouragement.

Personal Accountability: The capacity to take responsibility for one's own actions, conduct, obligations and decisions without excuses.

Personal Drive: A gauge of personal motivation to achieve, accomplish or complete tasks, goals or missions.

Personal Relationships: The importance of having and maintaining personal relationships and not just being seen as part of the team.

Persuading Others: The capacity to influentially present one's positions, opinions, feelings or views to others in such a way that they will listen and adopt the same view.

Planning and Organization: The ability to establish a process for activities that lead to the implementation of systems, procedures or outcomes.

Practical Thinking: The capacity to understand situations in a realistic, efficient manner and to achieve the desired results.

Proactive Thinking: The capacity to think ahead in order to realistically evaluate the consequences of current actions, processes and decisions.

Problem Solving: The ability to identify key components of the problem, possible solutions and the action plan to obtain the desired result.

Project and Goal Focus: The capacity to concentrate one's full attention on the project or goal at hand, regardless of distractions or difficulties.

Project Scheduling: The capacity to determine how long it will take to complete a project and to then efficiently break it down further into specific work time frames.

Quality Orientation: The capacity to maintain a focus on well-defined standards of excellence with regard to all aspects of responsibilities and tasks.

Realistic Expectations: The ability to set realistic time frames and well-defined standards of quality performance and production for others to follow.

Realistic Goal Setting for Others: The ability to define realistic and manageable goals for others using specific time frames and the resources at hand.

Realistic Personal Goal Setting: The ability to define realistic and attainable goals for one's self using specific time frames and the resources at hand.

Relating to Others: The capacity to understand and relate to others when communicating with them.

Resiliency: The ability to quickly recover from adversity.

Respect for Policies: The ability to understand, appreciate and have high regard for the rules, policies and procedures of the company.

Respect for Property: A measure of the level of respect and appreciation for the property that belongs to others or the company.

Results Orientation: The capacity to clearly and objectively understand and implement all variables necessary to obtain defined or desired results.

Role Awareness: The degree of a person's identity and awareness regarding his or her professional, social and personal roles.

Role Confidence: The capacity of maintaining confidence and self-reliance for fulfilling various professional and personal roles.

Self-Assessment: The capacity to objectively understand and evaluate one's self.

Self-Confidence: A measure of a person's assured self-reliance in his or her abilities.

Self-Direction: Having a clear vision of one's future objectives and the self-discipline and organization necessary to achieve them.

Self-Discipline and Sense of Duty: A measure of the level of devotion and commitment to one's own sense of obligation.

Self-Improvement: The measure of the quality of one's own internal motivation to improve.

Self-Management: The ability to prioritize and complete tasks in order to deliver desired outcomes within allotted time frames.

Self-Starting Ability: A measure of a person's ability to initiate tasks in order to fulfill responsibilities and commitments.

Sense of Belonging: A measure of how a person feels he or she fits into the surrounding world.

Sense of Mission: A measure of a person's sense of purpose in his or her life.

Sense of Self: A measure of a person's awareness of "who" they are - the ability to discern one's own self-worth.

Sense of Timing: The ability to do the correct thing at the correct time.

Sensitivity to Others: The capacity to understand and appreciate the value of other people with genuine concern for their needs, desires and feelings.

Status and Recognition: A measure of the importance of social status or prestige to a person's current role.

Surrendering Control: The capacity of a person to voluntarily surrender control and accept the authority of another person or group.

Systems Judgment: The capacity to understand and use systems such as knowledge, language, authority structures and logic, including one's ability to understand and work well within the context of established norms, rules, policies and procedures.

Taking Responsibility: A measure of the capacity to be answerable for personal actions.

Teamwork: The ability to cooperate with others to meet objectives.

Understanding Motivational Needs: The ability to understand and inspire others in such a way that gets them to act.

Using Common Sense: The capacity to be resourceful and apply good, practical, ordinary sense in whatever situations arise.